Race and Ethnicity

OTHER BOOKS OF RELATED INTEREST

Race and Ethnicity

Alma M. Garcia, *Book Editor*
Richard A. Garcia, *Book Editor*

David L. Bender, *Publisher*
Bruno Leone, *Executive Editor*
Bonnie Szumski, *Editorial Director*
Stuart Miller, *Managing Editor*
Brenda Stalcup, *Series Editor*

Contemporary Issues
Companion

Greenhaven Press, Inc., San Diego, CA

Every effort has been made to trace the owners of copyrighted material. The articles in this volume may have been edited for content, length, and/or reading level. The titles have been changed to enhance the editorial purpose. Those interested in locating the original source will find the complete citation on the first page of each article.

To our parents, Alma A. Garcia and Amado Garcia, and to my first mentor and longtime friend, Dianne M. Timbers, from Alma M. Garcia.

Library of Congress Cataloging-in-Publication Data

Race and ethnicity / Alma M. Garcia, book editor, Richard A. Garcia, book editor.
    p.   cm. — (Contemporary issues companion)
  Includes bibliographical references and index.
  ISBN 0-7377-0464-0 (alk. paper). —
ISBN 0-7377-0463-2 (pbk. : alk. paper)
  1. United States—Race relations. 2. United States—Ethnic relations. 3. Ethnicity—United States. 4. Pluralism (Social sciences)—United States. 5. Minorities—United States—Biography. I. Garcia, Alma M., 1952–   . II. Garcia, Richard A., 1941–   . III. Series.

E184.A1 R344 2001
305.8'00973—dc21   00-037138
                                                       CIP

©2001 by Greenhaven Press, Inc.
P.O. Box 289009, San Diego, CA 92198-9009

Printed in the U.S.A.

CONTENTS

Chapter 4: Personal Reflections on Race and Ethnicity

FOREWORD

In the news, on the streets, and in neighborhoods, individuals are confronted with a variety of social problems. Such problems may affect people directly: A young woman may struggle with depression, suspect a friend of having bulimia, or watch a loved one battle cancer. And even the issues that do not directly affect her private life—such as religious cults, domestic violence, or legalized gambling—still impact the larger society in which she lives. Discovering and analyzing the complexities of issues that encompass communal and societal realms as well as the world of personal experience is a valuable educational goal in the modern world.

Effectively addressing social problems requires familiarity with a constantly changing stream of data. Becoming well informed about today's controversies is an intricate process that often involves reading myriad primary and secondary sources, analyzing political debates, weighing various experts' opinions—even listening to first-hand accounts of those directly affected by the issue. For students and general observers, this can be a daunting task because of the sheer volume of information available in books, periodicals, on the evening news, and on the Internet. Researching the consequences of legalized gambling, for example, might entail sifting through congressional testimony on gambling's societal effects, examining private studies on Indian gaming, perusing numerous websites devoted to Internet betting, and reading essays written by lottery winners as well as interviews with recovering compulsive gamblers. Obtaining valuable information can be time-consuming—since it often requires researchers to pore over numerous documents and commentaries before discovering a source relevant to their particular investigation.

Greenhaven's Contemporary Issues Companion series seeks to assist this process of research by providing readers with useful and pertinent information about today's complex issues. Each volume in this anthology series focuses on a topic of current interest, presenting informative and thought-provoking selections written from a wide variety of viewpoints. The readings selected by the editors include such diverse sources as personal accounts and case studies, pertinent factual and statistical articles, and relevant commentaries and overviews. This diversity of sources and views, found in every Contemporary Issues Companion, offers readers a broad perspective in one convenient volume.

In addition, each title in the Contemporary Issues Companion series is designed especially for young adults. The selections included in every volume are chosen for their accessibility and are expertly edited in consideration of both the reading and comprehension levels of the audience. The structure of the anthologies also enhances accessibility. An introductory essay places each issue in context and provides helpful facts such as historical background or current statistics and legislation that pertain to the topic. The chapters that follow organize the material and focus on specific aspects of the book's topic. Every essay is introduced by a brief summary of its main points and biographical information about the author. These summaries aid in comprehension and can also serve to direct readers to material of immediate interest and need. Finally, a comprehensive index allows readers to efficiently scan and locate content.

The Contemporary Issues Companion series is an ideal launching point for research on a particular topic. Each anthology in the series is composed of readings taken from an extensive gamut of resources, including periodicals, newspapers, books, government documents, the publications of private and public organizations, and Internet websites. In these volumes, readers will find factual support suitable for use in reports, debates, speeches, and research papers. The anthologies also facilitate further research, featuring a book and periodical bibliography and a list of organizations to contact for additional information.

A perfect resource for both students and the general reader, Greenhaven's Contemporary Issues Companion series is sure to be a valued source of current, readable information on social problems that interest young adults. It is the editors' hope that readers will find the Contemporary Issues Companion series useful as a starting point to formulate their own opinions about and answers to the complex issues of the present day.

INTRODUCTION

In his classic work *The Souls of Black Folk,* published in 1903, renowned African American scholar W.E.B. Du Bois predicted that the issue of race would become the major problem of the twentieth century. Du Bois and other early scholars of race and ethnic relations in the United States documented the problems facing African Americans, Hispanic Americans, Native Americans, Asian Americans, and eastern and southern European immigrant groups such as Jews, Italians, and Poles. These immigrant communities faced urban poverty, unemployment, low education levels, inadequate health care, poor housing, and high crime rates. The sharp divisions between these groups and the rest of American society lessened gradually over time due to many factors, including social reform, economic advancement, gradual assimilation, and higher educational levels.

Racial and ethnic communities in the United States have always struggled with the tension between preserving an ethnic identity and assimilating into the larger community. Within ethnic neighborhoods in large cities, immigrants tried to preserve a sense of their native homeland and rear children who were proud of their ethnic heritage. On the other hand, immigrants and their second-generation offspring needed to assimilate to advance economically and socially. A gradual but not always smooth process of acculturation confronted all these groups. Today, although many racial and ethnic groups feel less pressure to abandon their ethnic roots, many find themselves mired in the same strife that plagued their ancestors.

Racial and ethnic tensions have always existed in the United States. Racial violence—particularly in the American South—has continued from the introduction of slavery to the present. Discrimination in education and politics, sanctioned by either law or custom, has commonly targeted Hispanics and African Americans. Native Americans have faced persistent poverty since the era of forced relocation to reservations that had little potential for economic opportunity. Until the early twentieth century, Asian Americans were denied citizenship and were prohibited from owning land. The noted philosopher and scholar of African American studies Cornel West sums up what his predecessor Du Bois said at the turn of the century: "Race still matters" in American society at the beginning of the twenty-first century.

Although the pages of American history document racial and ethnic conflict, individuals within immigrant communities have made long-standing efforts to overcome inequalities. Mexican immigrant communities in Texas, Native American communities in New Mexico and Arizona, African American communities in Mississippi and Alabama, and Japanese communities in California all have historical and contemporary legacies of individual and collective efforts to reform American society. The modern civil rights movement of the 1950s and 1960s set many precedents, notably the 1954 *Brown v. Board of Education* Supreme Court decision that declared segregation unconstitutional. The Civil Rights Act of 1964 stands as a major victory in protecting individual social and political rights. During the 1960s and 1970s, Hispanics and Asian Americans succeeded in winning legal cases that established the constitutional basis for bilingual education. Japanese Americans won restitution from the federal government for their internment in camps during World War II.

In light of the gains in rights these groups have attained and despite the continuation of racial and ethnic tensions, Americans in general tolerate and even empathize with diversity more than ever before. At the same time that newspapers and television news programs report racial strife, manifestations of racial and ethnic pride are exhibited in music, art, literature, film, and other areas of popular culture. Latino music is enjoyed by all groups and ages. Major museums organize exhibits by African American and Native American artists. In literature, Asian American, African American, Native American, and Hispanic writers fill the bookshelves of libraries and bookstores throughout the United States. Racial and ethnic diversity is celebrated as contributing to national character.

The goal of the editors when selecting the articles for this volume was to present a panoramic view of contemporary writings on racial and ethnic relations in the United States. The essays in chapter one, "The Nature of Race and Ethnicity," discuss the meaning and significance of race and ethnicity by focusing on social inequality. Chapter two, "Identity in a Multicultural Society," examines the development of individual and group identity and the patterns of intergroup relations. The writers included in chapter three, "Searching for the American Dream," raise a variety of questions related to the struggles, disappointments, hopes, and dreams of racial and ethnic groups in the United States. The last chapter, "Personal Reflections on Race and Ethnicity," includes autobiographical writings that illustrate the diversity of life experiences in communities of African Americans, Asian Americans, Native Americans, and Hispanic Americans. Intended to complement the other essays, these personal narratives provide readers with the human dimensions on the subject of race. By examining the wide range of viewpoints and opinions included here, readers are encouraged to reflect on the diversity of opinions presented and form their own ideas through an active engagement with the essays. The authors hope that this volume will contribute to the dialogue on developing a better understanding of race and ethnic relations in the United States.

CHAPTER 1

THE NATURE OF RACE AND ETHNICITY

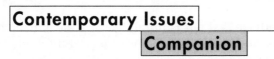

Contemporary Issues
Companion

DIVERSITY AND UNITY IN THE UNITED STATES: DEFINING TERMS

Joseph F. Healey

Joseph F. Healey is a professor of sociology at Christopher Newport University and has published the best-selling books *Race, Ethnicity, Gender, and Class* and *Statistics: A Tool for Social Research.* American society has confronted the issue of ethnic diversity and national identity since the Declaration of Independence. As a nation, Americans have struggled with questions of citizenship, intergroup relations, and racial and ethnic inequality. According to sociologist Healey, a discussion of such issues requires an accepted set of definitions as tools for understanding the racial and ethnic dynamics of the United States. In this article, Healey outlines key concepts, their definitions, and their usage in the study of race relations.

What does it mean to be an American? Recent controversies about immigration, cultural diversity, ethnicity, and race indicate that this question is far from settled. Many people fear our society will splinter into conflicting groups with no core of common values or language. How much diversity can we tolerate before national unity is threatened? How should we respond to the challenge of living in a diverse society (and a diverse world)? Should we stress our similarities and insist on conformity, and/or should we celebrate our differences and encourage diversity?

These questions are crucial but they are not new. They have been debated in one form or another over and over in our past. We are a nation of immigrants, and we have been arguing, often passionately, about exclusion and inclusion, unity and diversity, since the infancy of American society. Each wave of newcomers raises these issues once again, evoking the same fears and alarms, eliciting the same questions and concerns.

Our immigrant heritage and our cultural diversity have made us a nation of both groups and individuals. Some of us feel intensely connected with the groups to which we belong and identify closely with our heritage. For others the group connection is tenuous and distant.

Excerpted from Joseph F. Healey, *Race, Ethnicity, and Gender in the United States: Inequality, Group Conflict, and Power.* Reprinted with permission from Sage publications and the author.

Regardless of our subjective sense of the connection, our group memberships influence our lives and our perceptions. They help to shape who we are and how we fit in with the larger society.

The groups to which we belong have their own histories and, very often, different perspectives on the present and agendas for the future. Any discussion of the future of American group relations is unlikely to be meaningful, profitable, or even mutually intelligible without some understanding of this variety of viewpoints and experiences.

Some minority groups have been a part of U.S. society for centuries and still face systematic exclusion, widespread injustice, and oppressive inequality. In fact, there is considerable evidence that the problems of African Americans, Native Americans, Mexican Americans, and other groups are just as formidable today—or even more so—as they were a generation ago.

Other groups are more recent additions to the American mix and bring new traditions, new perspectives, and new questions. U.S. society is, at present, in a period of increasing diversity. Over the past three decades, the number of immigrants arriving in the United States each year has increased from fewer than 300,000 to more than a million. The current wave of newcomers includes groups from all over the globe.

As one simple way of gauging the dimensions of diversity in our nation, consider recent changes in the group makeup of American society. Table 1.1 shows the relative size of various groups in 1980 and 1993. Two different size projections for the year 2050 are also supplied. The highest growth rates, associated with Asians and Pacific Islanders and Hispanics, are the results of high birth rates as well as high rates of immigration.

Perhaps the most striking feature of the table is that white Americans declined in percentage of the population from almost 80% to less than 75% by 1993. As Table 1.1 makes clear, it will not take too many generations before "non-Hispanic whites" may be a numerical minority of the population. In fact, in some American cities such as Miami, they already constitute less than a majority of the population. Does this matter? What are the implications of these growth patterns for the future of our society? Can U.S. society deal successfully with this diversity of cultures, languages, and races? Does this changing group structure threaten the primacy of traditional white middle-class American values and lifestyles? Does it provide an opportunity to express other, equally legitimate, value systems? . . .

What Is a Minority Group?

Before we can begin to sort out the issues, we need common definitions and a common vocabulary for discussion. We begin with the term minority group, which is a bit misleading. Taken literally, the term has a mathematical connotation implying that the group so defined is small. In reality a "minority" group can be quite large and can even be a numerical majority of the population. Women, for example, are sometimes considered to be a separate minority group, but they are a numerical majority of the U.S. population.

Minority status has more to do with the distribution of resources and power than with simple numbers. . . . According to this definition, a minority group has five characteristics:

1. The members of the group experience a pattern of disadvantage or inequality.
2. The members of the group share a visible trait or characteristic that differentiates them from other groups.
3. The minority group is a self-conscious social unit.
4. Membership in the group is usually determined at birth.
5. Members tend to marry within the group.

Each of these defining characteristics is examined below. The first two—inequality and visibility—are the most important and are examined in greater detail in the following sections.

The first and most important defining characteristic of a minority group is inequality; that is, some pattern of *disability and disadvantage*. The nature of the disability and the degree of disadvantage are variable. At one end of the spectrum might be exploitation, slavery, and genocide (the extermination of the group). At the other end might be such slight irritants as a lack of desks in classrooms for left-handed students. . . .

Whatever the scope or severity, the pattern of disadvantage is the key defining characteristic of a minority group. Because the group has less of what is valued by society, a term synonymous with minority

Table 1.1 Groups in American Society

| | Percentage of the Population | | Projected Percentage of the Population in 2050 | |
	1980	1993	With No Immigration	With Immigration of 800,000 per Year
Asians and Pacific Islanders	2	3	4	10
Hispanics	7	10	18	22
Native Americans/ Eskimos/Aleuts	1	1	1	1
African Americans	12	12	17	14
Non-Hispanic Whites	80	74	61	52

Sources: 1980 data from the U.S. Bureau of the Census, 1993, p. 18; 1993 data and projections from Martin and Midgley, 1994, p. 9.

group is subordinate group. Inequality between minority and dominant groups might exist in their shares of wealth, jobs, housing, political power, police protection, health care, or schooling. More important, the pattern of disadvantage is the result of the actions of another group that benefits from and tries to sustain the existing arrangement. This group can be called the core group, the majority group, or the dominant group. Since it reflects the patterns of inequality and the power realities of minority group status, the last term will be most commonly used throughout this text.

The second defining characteristic of a minority group is the possession of some *visible trait or characteristic* that the dominant group holds in low esteem. The trait could be either cultural (e.g., language, religion, speech patterns, or dress styles), physical (e.g., skin color, stature, or facial features), or both. Groups defined primarily by their cultural characteristics are called ethnic minority groups. Examples of such groups would be Irish Americans or Jewish Americans. Groups defined primarily by their physical characteristics are racial minority groups, such as African Americans or Native Americans. Note that these categories can overlap. So-called ethnic groups may have distinguishing physical characteristics (e.g., the stereotypical Jewish nose) and racial groups often have cultural traits different from those of the dominant group (e.g., differences in dialect or religious values).

These traits, whatever they may be, are used to establish group boundaries and to identify members of the minority group. The traits operate like an outward sign that marks group membership and reinforces the patterns of disadvantage. The dominant group has (or, at one time, had) sufficient power to select the identifying characteristic, create and maintain the distinction between groups, and thus solidify a higher position for itself. These markers of group membership usually are not important in and of themselves but become crucial features of any dominant-minority relationship. Without such visible signs, it would be difficult or impossible to identify who was in which group.

Third, minority groups are *self-conscious social units,* aware of their differentiation from the dominant group and of their shared disabilities. The shared social status can provide the basis for strong intragroup bonds and a sense of fellowship. Also, the experience of being in a minority group can lead to a view of the world that is quite different from that of the dominant group and other minority groups. . . .

The fourth defining characteristic is that, in general, minority group membership is an ascribed status, one that is acquired at birth. The trait identifying minority group membership typically cannot be easily changed and minority group status is usually involuntary and for life.

Finally, minority group members tend to *marry within their own group.* This act is voluntary in part, but is sometimes dictated by the dominant group. It was only a generation ago in America that the law in many states forbade members of different racial groups to marry. The state laws against miscegenation, or interracial marriage, were declared unconstitutional in the late 1960s by the U.S. Supreme Court. . . .

Inequality

Inequality is the most important defining characteristic of a minority group. In fact, one reason minority groups are important is that they are associated with the general patterns of inequality in society. Minority group membership can affect access to jobs, education, wealth, health care, and housing. It is associated with a lower (often much lower) proportional share of valued goods and services and more limited (often much more limited) opportunities to improve one's situation.

Stratification, or the unequal distribution of valued goods and services, is a basic feature of society. Every human society, except perhaps the simplest hunter-gatherer society, is stratified to some degree. That is, the resources of the society are distributed so that some get more and others less of whatever is valued. Societies are divided into horizontal layers (or strata), often called social classes, which differ from one another in terms of the amount of resources they command. Many criteria (e.g., education, age, gender, or talent) may affect a person's social class position and his or her access to goods and services. Minority group membership is one of these criteria and it has had a powerful, even a controlling, impact on the distribution of resources. . . .

Minority Group Status and Stratification

There are at least three important relationships between minority groups and stratification. First, as we have already noted, minority group status affects access to property, prestige, and power. In the United States, this status has been a powerful determinant of life chances, health and wealth, and success.

Second, stratification and minority group membership, although correlated, are separate social realities. The degree to which one is dependent on the other varies from group to group. Today, for example, some American minority groups face formidable barriers to equality, whereas others, even groups that were massively victimized in the past, face only minor limitations on their social mobility.

Also, each minority group can be internally divided by the three dimensions of stratification. Different members of the same groups can have very different life experiences. Some might be economically successful, wield great political power, or enjoy high prestige even as the vast majority of their group languish in poverty and powerlessness. Of course, just as minority group members vary in terms of inequality, social classes can be split by ethnic and racial factors. . . .

Minority groups are not homogeneous. They can be divided along lines of wealth, prestige, and power, region of residence, religion, and any number of other criteria. One important source of variation within minority groups is gender. As a physical and biological trait, gender is like race; it is highly visible and can be a convenient way of judging people. It is common for societies to separate adult work roles by gender and to socialize boys and girls differently in preparation for these adult roles. In hunting-and-gathering societies, for example, boys train for the role of hunter, while girls learn the skills necessary for successful harvesting of vegetables, fruits, and other foodstuffs.

Gender roles and relationships vary across time and societies, but throughout history women have commonly occupied a subordinate status. Human societies are typically stratified on the basis of gender, with men claiming more property, prestige, and power than women. The societies of Western Europe and the United States, like most, have a strong tradition of patriarchy, or male dominance. In patriarchal societies, women possess many characteristics (e.g., a pattern of disadvantage based on group membership marked by physical characteristics) of a minority group.

Given these patterns of inequality and visibility, women could be, and in many ways probably should be, treated as a separate minority group. In this text, however, gender has been incorporated into the discussion of each minority group. This approach allows us to see that both the history and the present situation of members of minority groups vary by gender. Often, the bonds of gender are weaker or less controlling than the bonds of ethnicity or race. For example, the modern women's liberation movement has been largely a white, middle-class phenomenon. Although the movement raises issues of concern to all women, the major problem for minority group females is not just sexism but the entire system of racial and ethnic stratification that defines, stigmatizes, and controls the minority group as a whole. Thus, male and female minority group members often face different barriers and limitations in their dealings with the larger society. . . .

Key Concepts in Dominant-Minority Relations

This section introduces six concepts that are used to guide our analysis of minority-dominant relations. . . . *Prejudice, Discrimination, Ideological Racism, and Institutional Discrimination.* . . . We often discuss how individuals from different groups interact as well as how the groups themselves relate to one another. Even though the distinction between groups and individuals can be arbitrary and artificial (you can't have groups without individuals and vice versa), we need to distinguish between what is true for individuals (i.e., the psychological level of analysis) and what is true for groups or society as a whole (the sociological level of analysis). Beyond that, we must attempt to trace the connections between the two levels of analysis.

A further distinction on both the individual and group levels can be made. At the individual level, there can be a difference between what people think and feel about other groups and how they actually behave toward members of that group. For example, a person might express negative feelings about another group in private but deal fairly with members of that group in face-to-face interaction. Groups and entire societies may display this same kind of inconsistency. A society may express support for equality in its codes of law while simultaneously treating minority groups in unfair and destructive ways. For example, compare the commitment to equality stated in the Declaration of Independence ("All men are created equal") and the actual treatment of slaves, Anglo-American women, and Native Americans at that time.

At the individual level, we will refer to the "thinking/feeling" dimension as prejudice and the "doing" part as discrimination. At the group level, the terms *ideological racism* and *institutional discrimination* reflect a parallel distinction. Table 1.2 displays these four concepts, organized by level of analysis and dimension.

Prejudice is the tendency of an individual to think about other groups in negative ways and to attach negative emotions to other groups. Individual prejudice has two different aspects: the cognitive, or thinking, aspect and the affective, or feeling, part. A prejudiced person thinks about other groups in terms of stereotypes, generalizations that are thought to apply to members of the group. Examples of familiar American stereotypes include such notions as "Jews are stingy," "blacks are lazy," and "Irish are drunks." At the extreme, the prejudiced person believes that the stereotypes accurately characterize all members of the group. In addition to stereotypes, the prejudiced person experiences negative emotional responses to other groups, including contempt, disgust, and hatred.

People vary in their levels of prejudice, and levels of prejudice in the same person can vary over time. We can say, however, that people are prejudiced to the extent that they use stereotypes in their thinking about other groups and/or experience negative emotions in reaction to other groups.

The cognitive and affective dimensions of prejudice can be independent of each other. One person might think entirely in stereotypes but have little emotional reaction to other groups. Another person may feel strong aversion toward a group but be unable to articulate a clear mental image of that group.

Discrimination, unlike prejudice, refers to behavior and may be defined as the unequal treatment of a person or persons based on group membership. An example of discrimination would be an employer who does not hire an individual because he or she is African American (or Puerto Rican, Jewish, Chinese, etc.). If the un-

Table 1.2 Relationships Between Concepts

Dimensions	Level of Analysis	
	Individuals	Group/Societal
Thinking/feeling	Prejudice	Racism
Doing	Discrimination	Institutional discrimination

equal treatment is based on the group membership of the individual, the act is discriminatory.

Just as the cognitive and affective dimensions of prejudice can be independent, discrimination and prejudice do not necessarily occur together. Even highly prejudiced individuals may not act on their negative thoughts or feelings. On the one hand, in social settings regulated by strong egalitarian codes or laws (e.g., restaurants and other public facilities), people who are highly bigoted in their private thoughts and feelings may abide by the codes when they are in their public role.

On the other hand, situations in which prejudice is strongly approved and supported might evoke discrimination in otherwise nonprejudiced individuals. For example, in the American South during the height of segregation, it was usual and customary for white people to treat black people in discriminatory ways. Regardless of a person's actual level of prejudice, there was strong social pressure to conform to the patterns of racial superiority and participate in acts of discrimination.

Both the "thinking/feeling" dimension and the "doing" dimension can be found at the level of groups or entire societies. The former involves ideological racism, a belief system that asserts that a particular group is inferior. Whereas individual prejudice is an attitude, a set of feelings and stereotypes, racism is a set of ideas used to legitimize or rationalize the inferior status of a group. An example of a racist ideology would be the elaborate system of beliefs and ideas that attempted to justify slavery in the American South in terms of the innate racial inferiority of blacks.

Unlike individual prejudice, ideological racism is incorporated into the culture of a society, separate from the individuals who may inhabit the society at a specific point in time. It is a system of ideas that can be passed from generation to generation like any other part of the cultural heritage.

What is the relationship between individual prejudice and ideologies of racism? . . . We can make what is probably an obvious point: people socialized into societies with strong racist ideologies are likely to absorb racist ideas and be highly prejudiced. It should not surprise us that a high level of prejudice existed among whites in the antebellum American South or in other highly racist societies such as South Africa. At the same time, we need to remember that ideological racism and individual prejudice are different systems with different causes and different locations in the society. Racism is not a prerequisite for prejudice and prejudice may exist even in the absence of an ideology of racism.

For groups or societies, the "doing" dimension involves institutional discrimination, or patterns of unequal treatment based on group membership that are built into the institutions and daily operations of society. The public schools, the criminal justice system, and political and economic institutions can operate in ways that put members of some groups at a disadvantage.

Institutional discrimination can be obvious and overt. During the era of racial segregation in the American South, African Americans were prevented from voting. Elections and elected offices were limited to whites only until well after World War II by practices such as poll taxes and rigged literacy tests. The purpose of this blatant pattern of institutional discrimination was obvious and widely understood by black and white Southerners alike: it existed to disenfranchise the black community and keep it politically powerless.

At other times, institutional discrimination may operate in more hidden and unintended ways. If public schools use "aptitude" tests that are biased in favor of the dominant group, decisions about who does and who does not take college preparatory courses may be made on racist grounds even if everyone involved sincerely believes that objective criteria are being applied in a rational way. If a decision-making process has unequal consequences for dominant and minority groups, institutional discrimination may well be at work.

Note that whereas a particular discriminatory policy may be implemented by individuals, the policy is more appropriately thought of as an aspect of the operation of the institution as a whole. Election officials in the South during segregation or public school administrators today do not have to be personally prejudiced themselves in order to implement these discriminatory policies.

Institutional discrimination is one way in which members of a minority group can be denied access to valued goods and opportunities. That is, institutional discrimination helps to sustain and reinforce the unequal positions of racial and ethnic groups in the stratification system.

How are these four concepts related? A major thesis of this text is that *both racist ideologies and institutional discrimination are created in order to sustain the respective positions of dominant and minority groups in the stratification system.* The relative advantage of the dominant group is maintained from day to day by widespread institutional discrimination. Members of the dominant group who are socialized into communities with strong racist ideologies and a great deal of institutional discrimination are likely to acquire high levels of personal prejudice and to routinely practice acts of discrimination. The respective positions of dominant and minority groups are preserved over time through the mutually reinforcing patterns of prejudice, racism, and discrimination at both the individual and institutional levels.

RACE AND ETHNIC RELATIONS: MEASURING INEQUALITY

James M. Henslin

James M. Henslin is a professor of sociology at Southern Illinois University and has written extensively on gender roles and socialization, marriage, and families. His textbook *Introducing Sociology* has been widely recognized as a valuable contribution to introductory sociology courses. In the following selection, Henslin discusses two major areas in the study of race and ethnic relations. First, he outlines patterns of intergroup relations such as assimilation and pluralism. Second, he outlines the major sociological tools used to assess inequality in American society. This article is taken from Henslin's book *Social Problems*, which continues to be one of the major texts in the field.

Prejudice, discrimination, and racial violence are facts of life in the United States. Hostilities and tensions among racial and ethnic groups show up in street riots, racial disturbances in our schools, and the media-captivating activities of extremist groups. . . .

The United States certainly has no monopoly on prejudice and discrimination. On the contrary, they are common around the world. In northern Ireland, Protestants discriminate against Roman Catholics; in Israel, wealthier Ashkenazic Jews, primarily of European descent, discriminate against poorer Sephardic Jews, of Asian and African backgrounds; in Japan, the Japanese discriminate against just about anyone who isn't Japanese, especially the Koreans and Ainu who live there; and the disintegration of the former Soviet Union exposed the uneasy alliances among numerous racial/ethnic groups. Around the world, men discriminate against women. Discrimination—being singled out for unfair treatment—can be based on any number of characteristics, including age, race, sex, height, weight, health, income, and religious or political beliefs. (In contrast to discrimination, which is an action, prejudice is an attitude—a prejudging of some sort, usually in a negative way.)

Minorities, as sociologist Louis Wirth (1945) defined them, are groups of people who are singled out for unequal treatment on the

Excerpted from James M. Henslin, *Social Problems*, 4th ed. Reprinted with permission of Prentice-Hall, Inc., Upper Saddle River, NJ.

basis of their physical or cultural characteristics and who regard themselves as objects of collective discrimination. Wirth added that discrimination excludes minorities from full participation in the life of their society.

When used in reference to discrimination, the term "minority" does not necessarily mean a numerical minority in a society. In India, for example, a handful of British collectively discriminated against millions, and in South Africa, the group that had been relatively powerless, negatively stereotyped, and discriminated against is the black majority. Accordingly, . . . I shall refer to those who do the discriminating not as the majority but, rather, as the dominant group, those who have more power, greater privileges, and higher social status.

Minority groups come into being through two processes. The first is a consequence of expanded political boundaries. As anthropologists Charles Wagley and Marvin Harris (1958) note, small tribal societies have no minority groups (the exception is females . . .). In tribal societies everyone is "related," speaks the same language, practices the same customs, shares similar values, and belongs to the same physical stock. The second occurs when people with different characteristics move into a political unit. This can be forced, as with Africans brought to the United States, or voluntary, as with Turks moving to Germany to seek work.

Whether it is expanding political boundaries or people moving into a political boundary, minorities come into existence when diverse groups are brought under the control of one state organization. People with different customs, languages, values, and physical characteristics become members of a single social entity. Unified by shared physical and cultural traits, some groups use political power to discriminate against those with different traits. The losers in this power struggle are forced into minority group status, while the winners enjoy the higher status and greater privileges afforded by their political dominance.

Wagley and Harris identify five characteristics that minorities share worldwide:

1. Minorities are unequally treated by the dominant group.
2. The physical or cultural traits that distinguish minorities are held in low esteem by the dominant group.
3. Minorities tend to feel strong group solidarity because of their physical or cultural traits—and the disabilities these traits entail.
4. Membership in a minority group is not voluntary but comes through birth.
5. By choice or necessity, members of a minority group tend to marry within their group.

Experiencing collective discrimination, sharing cultural or physical traits, and marrying within their own group lead to a shared sense of identity—in some instances, even to a sense of common destiny. Such shared experiences, however, do not mean that all members of a minority group are united in their goals. Louis Wirth (1945) identified four different objectives that minority groups may have:

1. *Pluralism*: With pride in their own distinctiveness and toleration for differences in others, they desire to live peacefully side by side with the dominant group.
2. *Assimilation*: Focusing on the culture they share with the dominant group and desiring to participate in society fully, members of the minority prefer to be absorbed into the larger society and to be treated simply as individuals rather than as members of a special group.
3. *Secession*: Desiring both cultural and political independence, the minority seeks to separate itself nationally.
4. *Militancy*: Convinced of its own superiority, the minority group desires a total reversal in status and seeks to dominate the society.

Dominant groups around the world also differ in their goals and attitudes toward minorities. As illustrated in Figure 1, sociologists George Simpson and J. Milton Yinger (1972) identified five policies adopted by dominant groups. As you can see, these sometimes parallel and sometimes oppose the aims of minorities.

I. *Assimilation*. Assimilation represents the attempt to "eliminate" the minority by absorbing it into the mainstream culture. In its more severe form, *forced* assimilation, the dominant group refuses to allow the minority to practice its religion, speak its language, or follow its customs. In the former Soviet Union, this was how the Russians treated its Armenian citizens. *Permissible* assimilation, in contrast, permits the minority to adopt the dominant group's patterns in its own

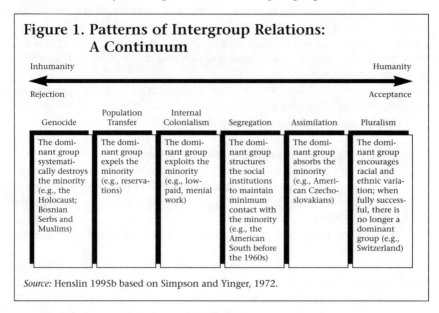

Figure 1. Patterns of Intergroup Relations: A Continuum

Inhumanity   Humanity

⬅━━➡

Rejection   Acceptance

Genocide	Population Transfer	Internal Colonialism	Segregation	Assimilation	Pluralism
The dominant group systematically destroys the minority (e.g., the Holocaust; Bosnian Serbs and Muslims)	The dominant group expels the minority (e.g., reservations)	The dominant group exploits the minority (e.g., low-paid, menial work)	The dominant group structures the social institutions to maintain minimum contact with the minority (e.g., the American South before the 1960s)	The dominant group absorbs the minority (e.g., American Czechoslovakians)	The dominant group encourages racial and ethnic variation; when fully successful, there is no longer a dominant group (e.g., Switzerland)

Source: Henslin 1995b based on Simpson and Yinger, 1972.

way and at its own speed. In Brazil, for example, various racial and ethnic groups intermarry, supported by an ideology that favors an eventual blending of its diverse racial types into a "Brazilian stock." The assimilation policy in the United States has been an interesting one—encouraging cultural minorities to give up their differences, while expecting racial minorities to maintain their physical differences by marrying within their own groups.

II. *Pluralism.* Some dominant groups permit or even encourage cultural variation, or pluralism. After their revolution, Russian communists supported both racial and cultural pluralism. They guaranteed minorities the right to practice their beliefs and customs, declaring them "free and inviolable." Later the Soviets turned to a policy of forced assimilation and systematically ridiculed, attacked, and dispersed minorities. The United States has often followed a pluralistic path. A "hands-off" policy toward immigrant associations and foreign-language newspapers has prevailed, and both racial and cultural minorities have been able to assert their individualism. . . . Probably the most outstanding example of a successful policy of pluralism is Switzerland, where the cultural differences of the French, Italian, and German Swiss, who have kept their own languages, are overridden by their political and economic unity. Living peacefully together, none of these groups can any longer be called a minority.

III. *Population transfer.* In *direct* population transfer, the minority is forced to leave. Examples include King Ferdinand and Queen Isabella (who financed Columbus's voyage to America) driving the Jews out of Spain and the relocation of Americans of Japanese descent into camps during World War II. *Indirect population transfer* means making life so unbearable for members of a minority that they "choose" to leave. Under the bitter conditions of czarist Russia, for example, millions of Jews made this "choice."

IV. *Continued subjugation.* This occurs when the dominant group wants to keep the minority "in its place," that is, subservient and exploitable. An example is provided by South Africa: When the whites were in political control, they despised the blacks and their customs, but they found their presence necessary. As Simpson and Yinger (1972) succinctly put the matter, who else would do all the hard work? A small dominant group of whites subjugated the black majority through a policy known as apartheid, the enforced segregation of blacks and whites in almost all spheres of life. Eventually, because of international sanctions, apartheid was dismantled.

V. *Genocide.* Hatred of a minority group or the desire to appropriate its resources sometimes leads the dominant group to turn to a policy of extermination, or genocide. Perhaps the most infamous example is that of the Nazis, who in a systematic policy, known to them as *Entlösung* but to us as the Holocaust, set up death camps to exterminate minorities. Between 1933 and 1945 they slaughtered about 6 million

Jews, a quarter of a million Gypsies, hundreds of thousands of Slavs, and unknown numbers of homosexuals, communists, and physically deformed or mentally ill persons whom Hitler did not consider "pure" enough to be part of his mythical Aryan race.

Hitler was convinced that race—the inherited physical characteristics that visibly identify a group of people—was reality. He believed that a race he called the Aryans was responsible for the cultural achievements of Europe. These tall, fair-skinned, blond-haired people—the "superrace"—contained within their biology the stuff that made them inherently superior. Consequently, they were both biologically and culturally destined to establish a higher culture, a new world order. This required subjugating inferior races to perform tasks too lowly for the Aryans, avoiding the "racial contamination" that breeding with inferior races would engender, and isolating or destroying races that might endanger Aryan culture.

While most people today find Hitler's racial ideas bizarre, in the 1930s both laypeople and the scientific community took them seriously. Many biologists and anthropologists of that period, for example, supported the idea that some races were inherently superior to others. It is perhaps not surprising that these scientists always concluded that Caucasians were the superior race, for they themselves were Caucasian. . . .

While ideas of racial superiority that justify one group's rule over another are considerably less popular today, the idea of race is still a social reality. People regularly identify others on the basis of appearance, classify them into racial groups, and treat them accordingly. Everyone has ideas, opinions, and attitudes on this topic, and these strongly held feelings and beliefs continue to motivate people's behavior. In this sense, then, race is still reality.

From the point of view of modern biology, however, pure race is not reality but a historical myth. People show so great a mixture of physical characteristics—in skin color, hair texture, nose shape, head shape, height, eye color, and so on—that the idea of pure races cannot be substantiated. Instead, human characteristics flow endlessly into one another, and the minute gradations inevitably make arbitrary any attempt to draw sharp lines. Large groupings of humans, however, can be classified by blood type and gene frequencies. Depending on the criteria they choose to use, biologists and anthropologists can develop arbitrary listings that contain any number of "races." Ashley Montagu (1964), a physical anthropologist, points out that some scientists have classified humans into as many as 2,000 "races," others as few as two. Montagu (1960) himself classifies humans into 40 "racial" groups.

Because the idea is so embedded in our culture, race is a social reality that social scientists must confront. As sociologists deal with this topic, they often prefer to avoid a term so imprecise and sometimes

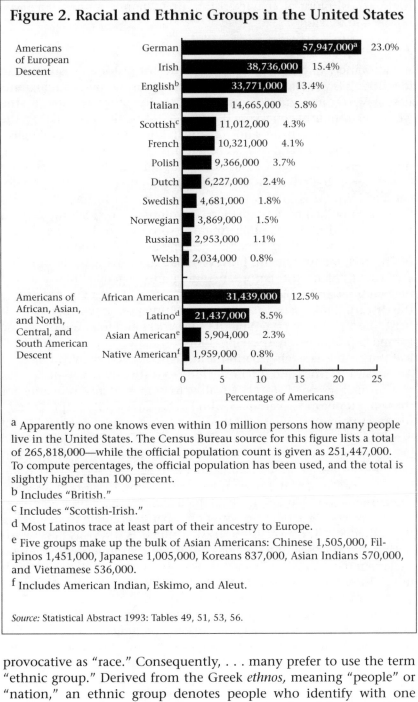

Figure 2. Racial and Ethnic Groups in the United States

Americans of European Descent

German	57,947,000[a]	23.0%
Irish	38,736,000	15.4%
English[b]	33,771,000	13.4%
Italian	14,665,000	5.8%
Scottish[c]	11,012,000	4.3%
French	10,321,000	4.1%
Polish	9,366,000	3.7%
Dutch	6,227,000	2.4%
Swedish	4,681,000	1.8%
Norwegian	3,869,000	1.5%
Russian	2,953,000	1.1%
Welsh	2,034,000	0.8%

Americans of African, Asian, and North, Central, and South American Descent

African American	31,439,000	12.5%
Latino[d]	21,437,000	8.5%
Asian American[e]	5,904,000	2.3%
Native American[f]	1,959,000	0.8%

Percentage of Americans

[a] Apparently no one knows even within 10 million persons how many people live in the United States. The Census Bureau source for this figure lists a total of 265,818,000—while the official population count is given as 251,447,000. To compute percentages, the official population has been used, and the total is slightly higher than 100 percent.

[b] Includes "British."

[c] Includes "Scottish-Irish."

[d] Most Latinos trace at least part of their ancestry to Europe.

[e] Five groups make up the bulk of Asian Americans: Chinese 1,505,000, Filipinos 1,451,000, Japanese 1,005,000, Koreans 837,000, Asian Indians 570,000, and Vietnamese 536,000.

[f] Includes American Indian, Eskimo, and Aleut.

Source: Statistical Abstract 1993: Tables 49, 51, 53, 56.

provocative as "race." Consequently, . . . many prefer to use the term "ethnic group." Derived from the Greek *ethnos,* meaning "people" or "nation," an ethnic group denotes people who identify with one another on the basis of their ancestry and cultural heritage. Their sense of belonging centers around such factors as their unique customs, foods, physical characteristics, dress, family names, language, music, and religion. . . .

The Scope of the Problem

A wide variety of ethnic groups with different histories, customs, and identities has populated the United States. Our nation of immigrants has drawn ethnic groups from nearly every other country in the world. Contributing the largest numbers were the Irish during the mid-1800s, the Germans and Italians in the late 1800s, the English from the 1600s on, and African Americans brought in as slaves beginning in 1619. The largest groups of immigrants are listed in Figure 2.

Whatever their background, the immigrants confronted Anglo-conformity; that is, they were expected to maintain English institutions (as modified by the American Revolution), to speak the English language, and to adopt other Anglo-Saxon ways of life. The United States was supposedly destined to become a slightly modified version of England. Many thought, however, that an evolving American society would "melt" the European immigrants together into a totally new cultural and biological blend. The United States would become the first truly international nation, a melting pot, in which, as sociologist Milton Gordon (1964) put it, "the stocks and folkways of Europe [would be], figuratively speaking, indiscriminately mixed in the political pot of the emerging nation and melted together by the fires of American influence and interaction into a distinctly new type."

The melting pot became a reality to some extent—primarily for those of European backgrounds who largely gave up their specific ethnic identities and merged into the mainstream culture. But the idea of a melting pot was as much ideology—a set of defensive values and beliefs—as it was reality, for many groups retained their unique cultures and ethnic identities. Immigrants who have arrived in large numbers in recent years, the most noteworthy being those from Mexico, Cuba, Haiti, and Vietnam, have retained a distinctive ethnic identity.

The concept of a melting pot is only partly accurate in describing the United States, concealing at least as much as it reveals. It is worth noting that the "melting pot" did not mean that Americans of Anglo background intended for non-Anglos to become part of a "biological mix." To enforce their ideas of racial purity, they even passed laws prohibiting blacks and whites from marrying.

Upon arrival, each group typically confronted prejudice, and new groups arriving still do. Helping to keep prejudice alive are stereotypes, exaggerated beliefs consisting of unfounded generalizations of what people are like. For example, the Irish immigrants were despised by many who had preceded them (especially the English) as dirty, lazy, untrustworthy drunkards. The Irish survived such stereotyping and joined the mainstream of society, becoming "respectable." Today, both whites and minorities hold debasing stereotypes of one another.

Prejudice and stereotyping are not necessarily social problems. Diverse groups can peacefully coexist, even if they are prejudiced against one another. If people are upset because prejudice deprives minorities of the rights to which their citizenship entitles them, however, a social problem exists. And if prejudice turns into hatred, discrimination, and conflict, these are the hallmarks of severely troubled ethnic relations.

As with other social problems, however, exactly what is problematic about ethnic relations depends on one's vantage point. . . . For members of the Ku Klux Klan and their sympathizers, minorities themselves create the social problem. They think that minority group members who mix with the mainstream and make economic, social, and political gains do so at the expense of whites.

Others feel that prejudice and discrimination have thwarted the fulfillment of the American ideal of equality of opportunity. This failure of principles guaranteed by the Constitution, along with the harm and tensions it engenders, is seen as the social problem of ethnic relations. This selection presents the social problem of race and ethnic relations from this perspective—as discrimination that hurts people.

I wish to note, first, that *discrimination can occur without awareness on the part of those doing the discriminating or those who are objects of discrimination.* An example is coronary bypass. This surgery is fairly common in the United States, with about 200,000 operations performed each year. Mark Wenneker and Arnold Epstein (1989), two physicians, became curious about the possibility of racial discrimination, and they studied all patients admitted to Massachusetts hospitals for circulatory diseases or chest pain. After allowing for age, sex, payer (insurance, individual, etc.), and income, they found substantial racial inequalities: Whites were 89 percent more likely to be given coronary bypass surgery. The particular interracial dynamics that underlie medical decisions being made on the basis of race are unknown.

There are a number of ways of measuring the harm that discrimination causes, for it leaves hardly an area of its victims' lives untouched. Indeed, discrimination is perhaps the central fact of life for a member of a minority group. It is most readily visible, however, in the area of economic well-being. As shown in Table 1, family incomes of African Americans and Latinos are substantially less than those of whites. The average Latino family income is only 61 percent of the average white income, and the income of the average African-American family is only about 54 percent of that of whites.

Another way to measure economic position is the unemployment rate. As Table 1 shows, substantial inequalities are apparent in this indicator as well. The unemployment rate for both African Americans and Latinos is about double that of whites. Unemployment rates are even more startling if we focus on particular segments of the minority

Table 1. Indicators of Relative Economic Well-Being

	Median Family Income		Unemployment Rate		Poverty Level	
	Median Family Income	Percentage of White Median Family Income	Percentage Who Are Unemployed	Percentage of White Unemployment Rate	Percentage Below Poverty Level	Percentage of White Poverty Level
White	$38,909		4%		9%	
Hispanic	$23,912	61%	7%	175%	29%	322%
Black	$21,161	54%	8%	200%	31%	344%

Source: Statistical Abstract 1994: Tables 49, 53.

population. Among young African-American urban males, for instance, unemployment may run 50 percent. . . . Another indicator of relative economic position is the proportion of a group whose income is below the federally defined poverty level. Table 1 shows that both African Americans and Latinos are more than three times as likely as whites to be poor.

These measures of economic well-being—poverty, unemployment, and income—all show that the average African American and Latino are substantially worse off than the average white. But what is the significance of these statistics? Behind the cold, abstract numbers are living people, people whose lives are adversely affected because they were born in a society where ethnicity and color are paramount factors in determining an individual's fate.

The significance of income in the United States can hardly be overstated. Income is the key that opens or closes the door to success in our society. We are not simply discussing the decisions middle-class people might make about their material well-being. . . .

The consequences of ethnic discrimination translate into matters of life and death. Note that an African-American baby has *more than twice* the chance of dying as does a white baby; that the chances of a mother dying during childbirth are *three* times higher for African-American women; that, on average, African-American females live about six years less than white females; and African-American males die almost eight years younger than white males. As measured by number of days sick, African Americans are unhealthier than whites. In short, higher income provides better nutrition, housing, and medical care—and a longer life.

People who are prejudiced think that minority groups are to blame for the conditions they experience. Extremists ascribe the blame to inborn racial or ethnic inferiority. Others, somewhat less extreme, place the blame on characteristics acquired by the group, such as laziness. Whether they are considered innate (genetic) or acquired (cultural), racists turn matters up-side down: They place blame on the group that is discriminated against instead of on the discrimination.

To understand the effects of discrimination, we need to move beyond thinking in terms of individual discrimination, one person treating another negatively on the basis of the latter's race or ethnicity. While individual discrimination certainly creates problems for people, it is primarily a problem to be solved by individuals. The law, however, may become involved if on the basis of race or ethnicity a person illegally withholds something, such as employment or housing.

Sociologists, however, encourage us to move beyond individual situations and to think in broader terms. They point to institutional discrimination as the essence of the social problem. This is discrimination built into the social system to oppress whole groups. For example, for generations whites denied African Americans the right to vote, to join labor unions, to work at higher-paying and more prestigious jobs, to attend the better schools, or to receive medical treatment at the better hospitals. The group that controls the great majority of real estate sales in the United States, the National Association of Real Estate Boards (NAR), used to openly support racial discrimination as a basic *moral* principle. Its 1924 code of ethics stated:

> A Realtor should never be instrumental in introducing into a neighborhood . . . members of any race or nationality, or individuals whose presence will clearly be detrimental to property values in that neighborhood.

This policy was supported by the federal government. The Federal Housing Authority (FHA) told developers of subdivisions that if they wanted loans to develop housing they had to include rules against nonwhites. Even after World War II, the FHA denied loans to anyone who would "unsettle a neighborhood." The FHA manual stated:

> If a neighborhood is to retain stability, it is necessary that properties shall continue to be occupied by the same social and racial classes.

The federal government changed its position and, under pressure, in 1950 the NAR deleted the reference to race or nationality. This formal change did not affect its practice, however, and the NAR continued to discriminate. Finally, in 1972 the NAR adopted a pro–fair-housing position.

The conspiracy by some realtors to withhold desirable housing from African Americans continues to this day, although it is no longer official NAR policy or practice. The major techniques in use are

1. *Double listings*. Realtors keep two sets of records, one with housing for "desirable" clients and the other for "undesirables."
2. *Double pricing*. Realtors inflate the official price and tell minori-

ties it is firm, while informing those considered "right for the neighborhood" that they can purchase the house for several thousand dollars less.

3. *Private listings.* Realtors do not advertise but merely handle properties informally "for friends," letting only the "right" people learn of properties for rent or sale by word of mouth.

Figure 3. Race/Ethnicity and Mortgages: An Example of Institutional Discrimination

The figures refer to applicants for conventional mortgages. Although applicants for government-backed mortgages had lower overall rates of rejection, the identical pattern showed up for all income groups. Median income is the income of each bank's local area.

In 1990, the Federal Reserve Board gathered data on the lending practices of 9,300 financial institutions across the United States. As shown here, loan applicants who have the same income do not receive the same treatment. Note how much more likely banks are to turn down minorities.

This study illustrates institutional (or systemic) discrimination. The figures clearly indicate that being turned down for a mortgage is not simply a matter of an individual banker here and there discriminating, but, rather, constitutes a nationwide practice. Rejection by race or ethnicity holds regardless of the individual's income or geographic area.

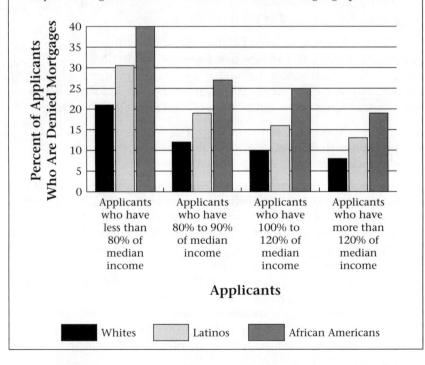

4. *Steering.* Realtors "steer" clients to "racially appropriate" neighborhoods so "everyone will be happy."

Discrimination in mortgage lending also continues. When two applicants for a mortgage are identical in debts, loan size relative to
income, and even characteristics of the property they want to buy,
African Americans and Latinos are 60 percent more likely to be
rejected than whites. Figure 3 summarizes findings from over 9,000
U.S. financial institutions. Some accuse the study of being flawed, and
we must await further analyses of the data. . . .

The Future of the Problem

The . . . [latter] decades [of the twentieth century] have witnessed fundamental change in ethnic relations. Many patterns of ethnic discrimination, formerly taken for granted, are assumed by the majority
of Americans to be wrong today. While huge gaps still remain
between our ideals of equality and the reality of ethnic relations in
the United States, the direction is toward greater equality.

Before World War II, the U.S. government pursued a policy that
supported apartheid. After the tremendous dislocations that the war
caused, U.S. society was never again the same. One such dislocation
was the migration of hundreds of thousands of African Americans to
the North and their employment in the war industries. Following the
war, the federal government changed its policy of apartheid and
worked toward a policy of integration and social equality. This policy,
reaffirmed by the U.S. Supreme Court, has broken down many of the
institutional barriers that discriminated against minorities. It is
unlikely that these barriers will ever be reestablished.

Jobs will be the major battlefield on which the struggle for ethnic
equality is fought. The dilemma of affirmative action and "reverse discrimination" in the workplace will bulldog workers and employers.
Court rulings are destined to be controversial, for, of necessity, they
will disappoint one side or the other of those holding incompatible
philosophical positions.

For most Americans, education holds the key to the future. Regardless of ethnicity, those who advance farthest in education are destined
for the best jobs and the most highly satisfying lifestyles. Any group
that receives less schooling than the national average is likely to be
especially disadvantaged in our future technical society. Granted this
principle, the future looks brightest for Asian Americans and whites,
then for Hispanics, and much less so for African Americans and
Native Americans. Obviously, policies that encourage education need
to be developed.

A major dilemma that has emerged, one likely to be a burning issue
in the future, is the disturbing possibility that we have developed a
permanent underclass, an alienated group of people living primarily in
the inner cities who have little education, have been raised in single-

parent families, have high rates of violent crimes, drug abuse, disease, out-of-wedlock births, and death by murder—whose norms are self-defeating, if the goal is to become successful in mainstream society.

This group that has been left behind by the movement of minorities into middle-class life and middle-class neighborhoods becomes more disadvantaged with each passing year. Unless specific ways are found to reach them, the tragic cycle will perpetuate itself, with the children now being born in those conditions of poverty fated to repeat the lives of their parents. A primary structural factor that makes this sorry possibility likely is the continued decentralization of jobs—the movement of jobs from the city to the suburbs—which locks people in urban ghettos without means of transportation to those jobs or the financial ability to move closer to them.

The Los Angeles riots of 1992 that followed the not-guilty verdict of the white Los Angeles police officers who were videotaped beating an African-American traffic violator with their nightsticks will not be an isolated event. With the continuing cycle just outlined, riots—violent crowd behavior aimed against people and property—can be expected from time to time. The riots of 1992 were unusual in their extent—the bloodiest in U.S. history, with 60 people losing their lives, 2,300 people injured, thousands of small businesses burned, and about $1 billion of property destroyed. But with the frustration and anger at deprivation—being kept out of mainstream society, limited to a meager education, denied jobs and justice, and kept out of decent neighborhoods—it takes only a precipitating event for the sense of injustice to erupt in collective violence.

The rise of black nationalism and the resurgence of the Ku Klux Klan in recent years throw a wild card in ethnic relations. While goals of ethnic pride are laudable, any group, of any race or ethnicity, that preaches hatred will contribute to bitter divisions between the races, creating a climate which fosters violence among race/ethnic groups. This alarming potential, yet to be played out, holds the key to a fearful future.

Back in 1944, in his classic book *An American Dilemma*, Gunnar Myrdal contrasted the "American creed," as expressed in Christian ethics and the Declaration of Independence, on one side, with un-Christian and undemocratic behavior, on the other. Myrdal expressed his conviction that Americans would resolve the dilemma in favor of the higher values of the American creed, rather than the lower ones of discrimination and prejudice. That certainly is to be hoped.

Like successive waves, peaks of goodwill and high hopes in race/ethnic relations are followed by troughs of hatred and despair. The future will bring more of the same. Although we as individuals have little power or influence, our actions, collectively, are significant. In this sense, which C. Wright Mills realized, we can ask what we ourselves can do to help bring about a more positive future—or at the very least, not contribute to the hatred espoused by some.

THE PERSISTENCE OF RACIAL CONFLICT

Howard Winant

Howard Winant is a professor of sociology at Temple University and has served as director of the Latin American Studies Center. He is coauthor with Michael Omi of *Racial Formation in the United States from the 1960s to the 1980s*. In this essay, Winant argues that Americans will continue to face the challenge of persistent racial conflict and tensions in the twenty-first century. This selection outlines some of the major societal reforms that have been developed to lessen racial conflicts. Winant uses the African American civil rights movements to illustrate how reforms originate as a result of community activism. Nevertheless, Winant also points out that such reforms often lead to what he calls a conservative backlash. This backlash against implementing social policies that would lessen racial and ethnic inequality represents a major concern for America's future.

The contemporary United States faces a pervasive crisis of race, a crisis no less severe than those the country has confronted in the past. The origins of the crisis are not particularly obscure: the cultural and political meaning of race, its significance in shaping the social structure, and its experiential or existential dimensions all remain profoundly unresolved as the United States approaches the end of the twentieth century. As a result, the society as a whole, and the population as individuals, suffer from confusion and anxiety about the issue (or complex of issues) we call race.

This should not be surprising. We may be more afflicted with anxiety and uncertainty over race than we are over any other social or political issue. Racial conflict is the very archetype of discord in North America, the primordial conflict that has in many ways structured all others. Time and time again what has been defined as "the race problem" has generated ferocious antagonisms: between slaves and masters, between natives and settlers, between new immigrants and established residents, and between workers divided by wage discrimination, by culture, even by psychosexual antagonisms. Time and time again

Excerpted from Howard Winant, "Where Culture Meets Structure: Race in the 1990s," in *Race, Class, and Gender in a Diverse Society: A Text-Reader*, edited by Diana Kendall. Reprinted with permission from the University of Minnesota Press.

this "problem" has been declared resolved, or perhaps supplanted by other supposedly more fundamental conflicts, only to blaze up anew. Tension and confusion in postwar racial politics and culture are merely the latest episode in this seemingly permanent drama.

The persistence of racial conflict, and of the anxiety and confusion that accompany it, has defied the predictions of most government officials, social critics, and movement leaders. Until quite recently, mainstream economists and Marxists, liberals and conservatives, ethnicity theorists and nationalists all expected the dissolution of race in some greater entity: free market or class struggle, cultural pluralism or nation-state. That race remains so central a factor both in the U.S. social structure and in the collective psyche, ought—at the very least—to inject a bit of humility into the discourses of all these sages.

Thus chastened, let us enter once more into the thickets of *racial theory*. No task is more urgent today. The mere fact that basic racial questions are at once so obvious and so obviously unanswered suggests how urgent is further theoretical work on race. Still, one must approach the effort modestly, for the concept of race in some ways is as large as social theory itself.

My strategy here is to examine contemporary U.S. racial dynamics from the standpoint of *racial formation theory,* an approach developed specifically to address the shifting meanings and power relationships inherent in race today. I begin with some basic propositions about racial formation. Then I look at recent U.S. racial history, which, I suggest, is in transition from a pattern of domination to one of *hegemony*. . . .

Racial Formation Theory

Racial formation theory was developed as a response to postwar understandings of race. . . .

Racial formation theory looks at race as a phenomenon whose meaning is contested throughout social life. In this account race is both a constituent of the individual psyche and of relationships among individuals, and an irreducible component of collective identities and social structures.

Because race is not a "natural" attribute but a socially and historically constructed one, it becomes possible to analyze the processes by which racial meanings are attributed, and racial identities assigned, in a given society. . . . They are variable, conflictual, and contested at every level of society, from the intrapsychic to the supranational. Inevitably, many interpretations of race, many racial discourses, exist at any given time. The political character of the racial formation process stems from this: elites, popular movements, state agencies, cultural and religious organizations, and intellectuals of all types develop *racial projects*, which interpret and reinterpret the meaning of race.

The theoretical concept of racial projects is a key element of racial formation theory. *A racial project is simultaneously an interpretation, rep-*

resentation, or explanation of racial dynamics and an effort to organize and distribute resources along particular racial lines. Every project is therefore both a discursive and a cultural initiative, an attempt at racial signification and identity formation on the one hand, and a social structural initiative, an attempt at political mobilization and resource redistribution, on the other.

Interpreting the meaning of race is thus a multidimensional process in which competing "projects" intersect and clash. These projects are often explicitly, but always at least implicitly, political. Racial projects potentially draw both on phenomena that are "objective" or institutional and on those that are "subjective" or experiential. That such social structural phenomena as movements and parties, state institutions and policies, market processes, and so forth should be the source of political initiatives regarding race is hardly controversial. Racial formation theory, however, also finds the source of "projects" in less familiar social practices: in the manipulation and rearticulation of racial identities by their bearers, in the enunciation and transformation of racial "common sense," and in the various subversive, evasive, or parodic forms of racial opposition that closely resemble other forms of subordinated and postcolonial resistance. . . .

The Pre–Civil Rights Era

In the pre–civil rights era the U.S. racial order was maintained largely, though of course not exclusively, through *domination*. The most visible manifestations of this regime were all enforced by coercive means: segregation, racial exclusion, and physical violence culminating in extralegal terror. Periodic mob assaults on urban ghettos and barrios, deportations to Mexico in the Southwest, outright extermination and plunder of native peoples, anti-Asian pogroms, physical intimidation and murder by police, and of course the practice of lynching were all fairly characteristic of this epoch. It was not until well into the twentieth century, and even then only in certain areas where racially defined minorities had been able to establish themselves in large numbers and to initiate negotiations between the white establishment and minority elites, that a measure of "protection," and even patronage and political influence, were sometimes available. But even these gains were highly limited and fragile.

The Political Effects of the Black Movement

The black movement upsurge changed all that. It permitted the entry of millions of racial minority group members into the political process—first blacks, and later Latinos, Asian Americans, and Native Americans. It initiated a trajectory of reform that exposed the limits of all previously existing political orientations—conservative, liberal, and radical. With very few exceptions, all these currents had colluded with the denial of fundamental political rights to members of racially defined minorities.

The aftermath of this prodigious movement upsurge was a racial order in which *domination was replaced by hegemony*. Political mobilization along racial lines resulted in the enactment of reforms that dramatically restructured the racial order, reorganized state institutions, and initiated whole new realms of state activity. The achievement of the franchise, the establishment of limited but real avenues of economic and social mobility, the destruction of de jure segregation, the reform of immigration law, and the institution of a measure of state enforcement of civil rights were but a few of the movement's more dramatic accomplishments.

The Cultural Effects of the Black Movement

Furthermore, by transforming the meaning of race and the contours of racial politics, the racially based movements also transformed the meaning and contours of American culture. Indeed, they made identity, difference, the "personal," and language itself political issues in very new ways. They made mainstream society—that is, white people—take notice of "difference"; they created awareness not only of different racial identities, but also of the multiple differences inherent in U.S. culture and society. In short, the new movements vastly expanded the terrain of politics and transfigured U.S. culture.

Thus, where U.S. culture previously had been monolithic and stratified, and indeed racially segregated ("race records," segregated media, etc.), it now became far more polyvalent, far more complexly articulated. Without being able to argue the point fully, I think it fair to assert that since the mid-1950s—I am taking as a fairly arbitrary demarcating point the advent of rock and roll—U.S. culture has adopted a far more pluralistic cast. With respect to race, this means that genres of music, art, and language retain their bases in particular communities while at the same time "crossing over" with far greater regularity than was previously the case. Cultural differences coexist without requiring any overarching synthesis, yet partial syntheses take place continually. . . .

The Racial Reaction

The achievements and legacy of the black movement were hardly greeted with universal acclaim. Various currents on the right strongly objected to the extension of an egalitarian racial awareness into everyday, indeed personal, life. Strong opposition arose to confront the newfound assertiveness and proliferation of cultural difference that the movement had fostered.

The very successes of the movement, however, set limits on the reaction that succeeded it. Because such movement themes as equality, group identity, and difference could not simply be rolled back, it became necessary, from the late 1960s onward, to rearticulate these ideas in a conservative ideological framework of competition, individualism, and homogeneity. In other words, since the movement's introduction of new political themes could not be undone, opponents had to learn how to manage these political themes as well.

This is why today's political debates about racial inequality are dominated by charges of "reverse discrimination" and repudiation of "quotas," why demands for "community control" have reappeared in opposition to school desegregation, and why high government officials claim that we are moving toward a "color-blind society." Cultural debates are dominated by the right's *rejection* of difference and "otherness" (whether racial, gender-based, sexual, or anything else). The right's strong defense of "traditional values," of individualism, and of mainstream culture, its discourse about family, nation, our "proud heritage of freedom," and so forth betokens intense resistance to the very idea of a polyvalent racial culture. Many of the notes struck by the right in contemporary cultural debates over race are, shall we say, white notes. They reflect a deep-seated fear, perhaps unconscious and only occasionally expressed, of the racialized other who has plagued the European for so long.

The "Decentering" of Racial Conflict

By the end of the 1960s the emancipatory effects of the black movement upsurge . . . had been blunted by the racial reaction. Indeed, the dominant racial theory since World War II—ethnicity theory—which had once allied itself with the minority movements, reappeared as one of their chief theoretical antagonists: neoconservatism. Along with a reconstituted *far right,* the *new right* and *neoconservative* currents would emerge by the 1980s as three related but distinct right-wing racial projects.

Neoconservatism was largely an enterprise of intellectuals who sought to intervene in policy debates over race. Its chief concern was the threat to political and cultural traditions it discerned in racial minority demands for "group rights," or "equality of result." The *new right,* heir apparent of the 1960s backlash politics . . . , was a far more grass-roots movement, linked to the religious conservatism fostered by some sectors of Catholicism and Protestant televangelism; it was a key component of every Republican presidential victory from 1968 to 1988. The *far right* was a more motley crew, consisting of the traditional assortment of bigots and race baiters, but also newly possessed of a modernized wing. The latter emerged in the mid-1980s when Klan leader and Nazi David Duke decided to swap his robe for a sport coat, get a blow-dried haircut, and undergo extensive plastic surgery, both on his face and in his rhetoric.

On the left, the movement upsurge fell victim to its own success. In the effort to adapt to the new racial politics they themselves had created, racial movements lost their unity and raison d'être. Working within the newly reformed racial state was more possible, and confronting it more difficult, than during the preceding period. Opposition to the backward and coercive racial order of the South had permitted a tenuous alliance between moderate and radical currents of the movement, an alliance that the winning of civil rights reforms ruptured. The "triumph" of liberal democracy failed to placate radicals who sought not only rights, but power and resources as well. The conferring of rights did not appreciably change the circumstances of a black youth in North Philly or a *vato loco* in East Los Angeles. What was heralded as a great victory by liberals appeared to radicals as merely a more streamlined version of racial oppression.

By the late 1960s, then, the U.S. racial order had largely absorbed the challenge posed by the civil rights movement, responding effectively—from the standpoint of rule—with a series of reforms. At the same time it had largely insulated itself from the more radical of its racial challengers—for example, revolutionary Marxist and nationalist currents—by drawing upon traditional coercive means, but also by exploiting the ideological weaknesses inherent in these viewpoints.

Over the following two decades what remained of the movement evolved into two loosely knit racial projects, those of the *pragmatic liberals* and of the *radical democrats*. In the former group I include the surviving civil rights organizations, the liberal religious establishment, and the Democratic party. In the latter group I include "grassroots" organizations that continue to function at the local level, cultural radicals and nationalist groups that have avoided mystical and demagogic pitfalls, and survivors of the debacle of the socialist left who have retained their antiracist commitments.

This spectrum of racial projects, running from right to left, characterizes the United States today. In contrast to the earlier postwar period, the political logic of race in the United States is now "decentered," because the racial formation process operates in the absence of a coherent conflict. Only a comprehensive challenge to the racial order as a whole could generate such coherence. This decenteredness reflects not only the incomplete and fragmented character of the available racial projects, but also the complexity of contemporary racial politics and culture. None of the extant racial projects seems capable of presenting a durable and comprehensive vision of race. None can realistically address in even a minimally adequate way *both* the volatility of racial expression, meaning, and identities on the one hand, *and* the in-depth racialization of the social structure and political system in the United States. Indeed, such a totalizing vision of race may no longer be possible.

This decentered racial situation reflects an unprecedented level of societal uncertainty about race. The various racial projects listed here are merely efforts to advance one or another current, one or another political agenda, in a society wracked by racial anxiety and conflict. They may compete in the effort to construct a new racial hegemony, but they do not offer any real prospect of clarifying or resolving ambivalent racial meanings or identities. Despite occasional appearances to the contrary, the right-wing racial projects have no more gained racial hegemony than have those of the left. Rather, the state, business, media, and religious and educational institutions appear permanently divided, riven, inconsistent, and uncertain about racial conflicts and issues, much as we as individuals are confused and ambivalent.

Rethinking American History: The Need for a Multicultural Perspective

Evelyn Hu-DeHart

Evelyn Hu-DeHart is a professor of history, the chair of the Department of Ethnic Studies, and the director of the Center for Studies of Ethnicity and Race in America at the University of Colorado at Boulder. Hu-DeHart specializes in both Latin American history and Asian American studies. She has published two books on the Yaqui Indians of Mexico. In this article, Hu-DeHart examines the portrayal of minority groups such as Asian Americans and African Americans in U.S. history. The author calls for a "rethinking" of American history to include the struggles and triumphs of diverse racial and ethnic groups. Hu-DeHart calls for the further development of a multicultural education that will assure that future generations of Americans gain a richer understanding of their common national past.

• Neoconservative columnist George Will wishes to "affirm this fact: America is predominantly a product of the Western tradition and predominantly good because that tradition is good."

   • Neoconservative writer and editor Charles Krauthammer, in discussing the triumphalist march of Euroamericans in the "opening of the American West," otherwise known as Manifest Destiny, rationalized the genocide of millions of Native Americans and the forcing of survivors into "homelands" this way: "The real question is, what eventually grew on this bloodied soil? . . . The great modern civilizations of the Americas—a new world of individual rights, an ever-expanding circle of liberty, and twice in this century, a savior of the world from total barbarism."

   • Liberal historian of Camelot [the John F. Kennedy administration] fame Arthur Schlesinger asserts: "The U.S. escaped the divisiveness of a multiethnic society by a brilliant solution: the creation of a brand new identity. The point of America was not to preserve old cultures but to forge a new, American culture. 'By an intermixture with

Excerpted from Evelyn Hu-DeHart, "Rethinking America," in *Experiencing Race, Class, and Gender in the United States*, 2nd ed., edited by Virginia Cyrus. Reprinted with permission from the University of Minnesota Press and the author.

our people,' President George Washington told V.P. John Adams, 'immigrants will get assimilated to our customs, measures and laws: in a word, soon become one people.'" What these "immigrants" have in common, he continues, is "the Western tradition [which] is the source of the ideas of individual freedom and political democracy."

• Yale historian and undergraduate dean Donald Kagan lectured to a recent incoming freshman class: "Except for the slaves brought from Africa, most came voluntarily, as families and individuals, usually eager to satisfy desires that could not be met in their former homelands. They swiftly became citizens and, within a generation or so, Americans. In our own time finally . . . African-Americans also have achieved freedom, equality before the law, and full citizenship. . . . What they have in common and what brings them together is a system of laws and beliefs that shaped the establishment of the country, a system developed within the context of Western Civilization."

For many Americans educated and socialized in this dominant version of history, which is also the official view, the kind usually taught in our schools and universities, there may seem nothing wrong with the above statements. Indeed, for those Americans from European immigrant backgrounds, they probably ring true as accurate renditions of their shared historical experience in America's great melting pot. And they can justifiably take pride in having defined "our national identity" and "our national culture."

But there is also a problem with this version of national history for Americans of non-European heritage, some of whom have been here since the beginning. The fact of the matter is, the "our" in "our national identity" and "our national culture," and the "we" in "we the people" have also been historically exclusive. Bluntly put, there is another history that these "other" Americans have lived through. For one truth that is omitted in all these declarations of Western triumphalism is that, in thinking of the people who built America and benefitted from it, the images are overwhelmingly and almost exclusively those of European immigrants and their descendents.

African Americans, as even Donald Kagan had to concede, were not voluntary immigrants and not part of the national process in its formation. Indeed, in order to sidestep the obvious contradiction between slavery and "All Men are Created Equal," the Founding Fathers—all white male property owners—defined blacks and slaves as less than full human beings. And even if Kagan wishes to suggest that equality before the law has brought them nominal freedom and full citizenship, the reality is fraught with contradictions, as the Los Angeles uprising of May 1992 demonstrated all too clearly. The lingering and still institutionalized legacies of slavery, Jim Crow and legal apartheid which endure to this day, and which have left most African Americans still largely excluded or alienated from national life, cannot be blithely brushed aside, as triumphalists like Kagan would wish.

The Federal Government did not extend universal citizenship to Native Americans, the original inhabitants of this land, until 1924, shamed into doing so only after many had served and died in defense of this country during WWI. By then, most Native American peoples had lost their land and waters; many more had been destroyed by war and disease; still others [had been] removed and relocated far from their original homelands. Those not wantonly thrown into the streets of the inner cities to sink or swim on their own are still confined to reservations on desolate land in remote places, unemployed and unable to even scratch out a decent living, out of sight and therefore out of our conscience and consciousness. Is it any wonder that so many Native Americans actively protested Columbus Quincentenary celebrations, which to them appeared to be celebrating a history of genocide? As peoples whose relationships with the U.S. government were founded on treaty rights—a Western concept, after all—signed over the course of three centuries, and of which hundreds still remain on the books, they continue to insist on the sovereignty which signing treaties explicitly recognized. Why is it that triumphalists seldom speak of the sovereignty rights of Indian peoples in America, not to mention physical and cultural genocide committed against them in the name of Western democracy and freedom?

During the mid-19th century, America won by force, or bought at bargain basement prices vast chunks of land from Mexico, amounting to half of her national territory, and incorporated wholesale the vast, settled population of mainly Spanish-speaking mestizos (mixed Spanish-Indian heritage). Although, according to the Treaty of Guadalupe Hidalgo of 1848, they were promised citizenship and the right to retain their languages and cultures, these commitments have been honored mainly in the breach. Hardly voluntary immigrants to begin with, later arrivals from Mexico have more often been branded wetbacks and illegal aliens, seldom welcomed as legitimate immigrants. These brown-skinned Mexicans became a disenfranchised, disadvantaged minority group whose ranks would later be swelled by other forcefully incorporated, dark complexioned Spanish-speakers on American soil, such as Puerto Ricans, and [who would be] collectively known by the government-imposed term "Hispanics." Their distant connection with Catholic Spain and more recent connection with backwards, chaotic, Spanish-speaking Latin America (notably Mexico, Central America and parts of the Caribbean) render them problematic for purposes of racial classification. Are Hispanics white and European, or are most of them "different" by virtue of their religion (Catholicism), their language (Spanish), and their openly acknowledged legacy of miscegenation with Indians and blacks?

In this brief and admittedly oversimplified summary of the history of non-European peoples in the U.S., Asian/Pacific Americans remain to be considered. They indeed did migrate to America, but usually not so voluntarily, at least not in the 19th century when they first came as cheap laborers, lonely men for the most part unaccompanied by families and kin. If European immigrants to America were regarded as potential citizens, that unfortunately did not apply to Asians, for it was decided even before their arrival that they would have no access to citizenship. The U.S. Naturalization Law enacted in 1790, which remained in effect until 1952, specifically barred non-white immigrants from citizenship. Thus, when tens of thousands of Asian workers were brought to the American West during the 19th century to build the railroads, work the mines, clear virgin land for agriculture, they found themselves denied full political participation and social integration into this society. From 1882 to WWII, the Chinese also became the only people in American history singled out as an undesirable "race" that must be barred from further immigration to this country. During WWII, thousands of Japanese alien residents on the West Coast, [who] like the Chinese [were] ineligible for citizenship at the time, and their American born children were interned in camps behind barbed wire fences, even when not a single one of them had committed any act of disloyalty or sedition against their adopted country. The recent (since the late 1970s) elevation of Asian Americans to the status of "model minority," deemed superior to other minorities because of their apparent greater ability to assimilate white middle class virtues, cannot erase this long history of exclusion and unequal treatment.

In summary, from the vantage points of Native Americans, African Americans, Mexican Americans and Asian Americans, there is an underside of Western triumphalism in America that has not been acknowledged, recorded and told. The history of individual choice and freedom, and of democracy, described so eloquently and defended so passionately by Will, Krauthammer, Schlesinger, Kagan and many others, unfortunately does not speak to the truth as most of them and their predecessors in America have experienced it. These fundamental contradictions, between America's multiracial origins and growing multiracial reality on the one hand, and its still dominant self image as white and European on the other, between stated ideals of freedom and democracy for all, alongside a racialist social order that had historically relegated peoples of color to an inferior status as cheap labor, at best, and extraneous population at worst, but in any case not equal citizens, are what multicultural scholars have identified and attempt to resolve.

The noted historian Alexander Saxton, who happens to be white and male, says it well in his recent book, *The Rise and Fall of the White Republic*: "America's supposed openness to newcomers throughout most of its history has been racially selective. By the time of Jefferson and Jackson the nation had already assumed the form of a *racially exclusive democracy*—democratic in the sense that it sought to provide equal opportunities for the pursuit of happiness by its white citizens through the enslavement of African Americans, extermination of the Indians and further expansion at the expense of Indians and Mexicans. If there was an 'American orientation' to newcomers, it was not toward giving equal opportunity to all but toward inviting entry by white Europeans and excluding others. It is true that the United States absorbed a variety of cultural patterns among European immigrants at the same time that it was erecting a *white supremacist social structure. Moderately tolerant of European ethnic diversity, the nation remained adamantly intolerant of racial diversity. It is this crucial difference that has been permitted to drop from sight"* (emphasis added). Ethnic Studies and other scholars committed to the multicultural project are determined to bring this "crucial difference" back into focus. For contrary to the Western triumphalists, multicultural scholars assert that there was no national identity or national culture that embraced all Americans, thus no actual consensus or unity ever existed to be ripped apart by the newborn attention to the histories of the excluded groups. Rather, an official history has been shoved down the throats of those unable to speak for themselves until recently.

If triumphalists insist there is really only one viewpoint in history, or at least one true or "best" viewpoint, multiculturalists acknowledge multiple perspectives, depending on one's status and station in society that is determined in turn by race, class, gender, and other factors. The supportives, no one of which speaks the whole truth, can be in sharp conflict, may or may not be ultimately resolved, but in any case, together form a more complete picture of our national history, our national identity, our national culture. Accordingly, the New York State Dept. of Education Curriculum Task Force calls for a "new conceptualization of history, one that recognized multiplicity and contradiction instead of homogeneity and consensus as the basis of our national community." In short, multiculturalists would only concede that, once the triumphalists confront the past honestly, then acknowledge it openly, once those excluded Americans can come forth freely to reclaim their histories, and once institutional barriers to equal opportunity for all Americans have been removed, only then can we speak of seeking common ground, of forging unity and consensus. Until then, liberals like Schlesinger will plead for unity in vain, while rap singers speak greater truths to young blacks in the "hood" and Latinos in the barrio.

CHAPTER 2

IDENTITY IN A MULTICULTURAL SOCIETY

THE IMMIGRANT AND AMERICAN DEMOCRACY

Reed Ueda

Reed Ueda is an associate professor of history at Tufts University and has received awards and fellowships for his research on immigration from the American Council of Learned Societies and the Woodrow Wilson International Center for Scholars. Ueda has also served as a research editor for the award-winning *Harvard Encyclopedia of American Ethnic Groups*. This selection is taken from the author's book *Postwar Immigrant America*. In it, Ueda discusses the relationship between immigration and democracy. According to Ueda, America's legacy as a nation of immigrants continues to influence its identity and future. The author raises the question of whether groups from diverse backgrounds can develop a national identity in a democratic society. He concludes that when immigrants become citizens, they develop a common democratic goal: a belief in the constitutional guarantees that make the United States an integrated nation.

American government historically developed a flexible political and legal framework to accommodate the ethnic pluralism produced by mass immigration. Like the American economy and cultural institutions, it worked effectively to produce a cohesive nation for most of the twentieth century. As government expanded its role in combating discrimination, it brought increasingly fair opportunities for newcomers to rebuild their lives, thus furthering the social aspects of democracy. Beginning in the 1960s, however, the governmental framework for ethnic pluralism began diverging sharply from historic patterns, portending an uncertain future for American nationhood and democracy.

In the United States, weak and fluid boundaries between immigrant groups have been the historical key to national cohesion. Support for the principle of inclusive citizenship and nationality was the strongest guarantor of these boundary conditions. The American civic culture with its emphasis on individual rights provided a key support for the principle of inclusiveness. Another vital support came from the central historical role of immigration. The experiences of immigration, settlement, and the rebuilding of lives and communities shared by ethnic groups provided a common social foundation for a national identity that transcended group boundaries.

The strength of American civic identity over group boundaries derived, in addition, from the mechanisms of the American political system that limited the ability of groups to turn government into an instrument for advancing their interests as a group. The American system rested on a federal principle that had important consequences for the struggle for power among ethnic groups. The lack of political centralization meant that ethnic politics usually resided within local networks and operated through the historic regional constellations of groups: the Japanese vied for power with the Chinese in Honolulu, the Irish and Italians clashed in Boston, Mexicans and blacks jostled for control in Los Angeles. Because group politics was compartmentalized locally, it was difficult for interethnic struggles to penetrate the arena of national government. . . .

Learning American National Identity

For children of immigrants, schooling was the chief formal means of absorbing official American national identity. For most of the twentieth century, educators expected students to leave behind their ethnic identities when they entered the public schools, where they would gradually assume American national identity from their studies in history, literature, and social studies. Through readings and lessons students encountered an iconology of great figures in American history who personified the distinctive values of the country. They learned about the character of American institutions by learning about the history of building a democratic nation.

The schools constructed national history, ideals, and heroes as universal symbols available for adoption by all and sought to make learning about them inspirational. The children of immigrants learned about individual rights, self-government, and equality. The schools taught students to develop a self-image as individual citizens that served as the mold of national identity.

By cultivating ideological identification with the nation and its institutions, the public schools introduced subjective attachments to an official culture transcending ethnic identification. In this way schooling served as a force for creating a sense of nationality, assimilating immigrant groups by substituting civic inclusion for ethnic differentiation.

For most of the twentieth century, schools did not make it part of their mission to develop sensitivity to ethnic identity. In fact, educators sought to counteract the private culture of immigrant families and the public culture of ethnic neighborhoods. Indeed, these teachers were aided by textbooks and curricula that eschewed or discouraged ethnic identification. In their effort to promote an "American" style of classroom behavior and performance, some teachers were not above using intimidation. . . .

Education in national identity was highly variable in style and results. Many teachers failed to inspire their students, who were often passive and indifferent. The school's role in propagating the civic culture was probably most effective among groups that sponsored prolonged schooling and exceptional learning rates such as Japanese Americans and Russian Jews. These groups also shared a distance from official middle-class social and cultural values, making the effects of schooling significantly different from the influences learned at home.

Nevertheless, the classroom that focused on American national identity did help to democratize political consciousness and identity. . . . Ethnic students gained from schooling a new conception of their rights as American citizens that had the residual power to encourage their struggle for equality through adult life.

The educational history of the children of Japanese immigrants, the Nisei, supplies an insight into how schooling served not just as a means of supervised acculturation but as an outlet for projecting and claiming national identity. The second-generation Japanese in early twentieth-century Los Angeles were regarded as outstanding scholar-citizens in the public schools, receiving high marks in academic and citizenship grades and engaging actively in the institutional programs of the public school. Many Nisei probably felt that scholastic success demonstrated their American national identity and represented initial acceptance as citizens. . . .

Second-generation immigrant Americans from a variety of backgrounds found the symbols of official Americanism inspiring and politically powerful. The embrace of official Americanism and national identity was consistent with the empowerment of immigrant groups throughout national history. . . .

The Constitution and citizenship formed the guiding compass of group political agendas. The German philosopher of history Wilhelm Dilthey once argued that the great challenge of modern historiography was to determine how the many who constituted society were mobilized in concert by shared thoughts. Historian Oscar Handlin proposed a variation of Dilthey's assertion—that the United States early faced the key question of the modern world, how dissimilar people of different origins can act together under democratic conditions. The United States responded effectively to this problem because different peoples were unified by their adoption of the values of the Constitution. The shared pursuit of making the Constitution apply equally and fully to all people was a key aspect of the mutual endeavor of ethnic minorities intrinsic to American nation building.

REDEFINING AMERICAN SOCIETY: INTEGRATING A MULTICULTURAL PERSPECTIVE

Ronald Takaki

Ronald Takaki is a professor of ethnic studies at the University of California at Berkeley and is the author of the prizewinning book Strangers from a Different Shore. *Takaki is also the author of* A Different Mirror: A History of Multicultural America. *In this essay, Takaki discusses the persistence of racial and ethnic stereotypes in America. He suggests a redefinition of the term* American *to reflect the historical and contemporary experiences of diverse groups such as Asian Americans, Mexican Americans, African Americans, and Irish Americans. Takaki points out that American history must include views of the United States as a multiracial and multicultural society. In this selection, he stresses the need to focus on the historical conflicts and tensions that have characterized the histories of racial and ethnic groups in the United States.*

I had flown from San Francisco to Norfolk and was riding in a taxi to my hotel to attend a conference on multiculturalism. Hundreds of educators from across the country were meeting to discuss the need for greater cultural diversity in the curriculum. My driver and I chatted about the weather and the tourists. The sky was cloudy, and Virginia Beach was twenty minutes away. The rearview mirror reflected a white man in his forties. "How long have you been in this country?" he asked. "All my life," I replied, wincing. "I was born in the United States." With a strong southern drawl, he remarked: "I was wondering because your English is excellent!" Then, as I had many times before, I explained: "My grandfather came here from Japan in the 1880s. My family has been here, in America, for over a hundred years." He glanced at me in the mirror. Somehow I did not look "American" to him; my eyes and complexion looked foreign.

Suddenly, we both became uncomfortably conscious of a racial divide separating us. An awkward silence turned my gaze from the mirror to the passing landscape, the shore where the English and the

Excerpted from Ronald Takaki, *A Different Mirror: A History of Multicultural America.* Reprinted with permission from Little, Brown and Company.

Powhatan Indians first encountered each other. Our highway was on land that Sir Walter Raleigh had renamed "Virginia" in honor of Elizabeth I, the Virgin Queen. In the English cultural appropriation of America, the indigenous peoples themselves would become outsiders in their native land. Here, at the eastern edge of the continent, I mused, was the site of the beginning of multicultural America. Jamestown, the English settlement founded in 1607, was nearby: the first twenty Africans were brought here a year before the Pilgrims arrived at Plymouth Rock. Several hundred miles offshore was Bermuda, the "Bermoothes" where William Shakespeare's Prospero had landed and met the native Caliban in *The Tempest*. Earlier, another voyager had made an Atlantic crossing and unexpectedly bumped into some islands to the south. Thinking he had reached Asia, Christopher Columbus mistakenly identified one of the islands as "Cipango" (Japan). In the wake of the admiral, many peoples would come to America from different shores, not only from Europe but also Africa and Asia. One of them would be my grandfather. My mental wandering across terrain and time ended abruptly as we arrived at my destination. I said good-bye to my driver and went into the hotel, carrying a vivid reminder of why I was attending this conference.

Questions like the one my taxi driver asked me are always jarring, but I can understand why he could not see me as American. He had a narrow but widely shared sense of the past—a history that has viewed American as European in ancestry. "Race," [contemporary author] Toni Morrison explained, has functioned as a "metaphor" necessary to the "construction of Americanness": in the creation of our national identity, "American" has been defined as "white."

But America has been racially diverse since our very beginning on the Virginia shore, and this reality is increasingly becoming visible and ubiquitous. Currently, one-third of the American people do not trace their origins to Europe; in California, minorities are fast becoming a majority. They already predominate in major cities across the country—New York, Chicago, Atlanta, Detroit, Philadelphia, San Francisco, and Los Angeles.

This emerging demographic diversity has raised fundamental questions about America's identity and culture. In 1990, *Time* published a cover story on "America's Changing Colors." "Someday soon," the magazine announced, "white Americans will become a minority group." How soon? By 2056, most Americans will trace their descent to "Africa, Asia, the Hispanic world, the Pacific Islands, Arabia—almost anywhere but white Europe." This dramatic change in our nation's ethnic composition is altering the way we think about ourselves. "The deeper significance of America's becoming a majority nonwhite society is what it means to the national psyche, to individuals' sense of themselves and their nation—their idea of what it is to be American.". . .

What is fueling this debate over our national identity and the content of our curriculum is America's intensifying racial crisis. The alarming signs and symptoms seem to be everywhere—the killing of Vincent Chin in Detroit, the black boycott of a Korean grocery store in Flatbush, the hysteria in Boston over the Carol Stuart murder, the battle between white sportsmen and Indians over tribal fishing rights in Wisconsin, the Jewish-black clashes in Brooklyn's Crown Heights, the black-Hispanic competition for jobs and educational resources in Dallas, which *Newsweek* described as "a conflict of the have-nots.". . .

This reality of racial tension rudely woke America like a fire bell in the night on April 29, 1992. Immediately after four Los Angeles police officers were found not guilty of brutality against Rodney King, rage exploded in Los Angeles. Race relations reached a new nadir [low point]. During the nightmarish rampage, scores of people were killed, over two thousand injured, twelve thousand arrested, and almost a billion dollars' worth of property destroyed. The live televised images mesmerized America. The rioting and the murderous melee on the streets resembled the fighting in Beirut and the West Bank. The thousands of fires burning out of control and the dark smoke filling the skies brought back images of the burning oil fields of Kuwait during Desert Storm. Entire sections of Los Angeles looked like a bombed city. "Is this America?" many shocked viewers asked. "Please, can we get along here," pleaded Rodney King, calling for calm. "We all can get along. I mean, we're all stuck here for a while. Let's try to work it out."

But how should "we" be defined? Who are the people "stuck here" in America? One of the lessons of the Los Angeles explosion is the recognition of the fact that we are a multiracial society and that race can no longer be defined in the binary terms of white and black. "We" will have to include Hispanics and Asians. While blacks currently constitute 13 percent of the Los Angeles population, Hispanics represent 40 percent. The 1990 census revealed that South Central Los Angeles, which was predominantly black in 1965 when the Watts rebellion occurred, is now 45 percent Hispanic. A majority of the first 5,438 people arrested were Hispanic, while 37 percent were black. Of the fifty-eight people who died in the riot, more than a third were Hispanic, and about 40 percent of the businesses destroyed were Hispanic-owned. Most of the other shops and stores were Korean-owned. The dreams of many Korean immigrants went up in smoke during the riot: two thousand Korean-owned businesses were damaged or demolished, totaling about $400 million in losses. . . .

How did we get to this point, Americans everywhere are anxiously asking. What does our diversity mean, and where is it leading us? *How* do we work it out in the post–Rodney King era?

Certainly one crucial way is for our society's various ethnic groups to develop a greater understanding of each other. For example, how can African Americans and Korean Americans work it out unless they learn about each other's cultures, histories, and also economic situations? This need to share knowledge about our ethnic diversity has acquired new importance and has given new urgency to the pursuit for a more accurate history. . . .

African Americans have been the central minority throughout our country's history. They were initially brought here on a slave ship in 1619. Actually, these first twenty Africans might not have been slaves; rather, like most of the white laborers, they were probably indentured servants. The transformation of Africans into slaves is the story of the "hidden" origins of slavery. How and when was it decided to institute a system of bonded black labor? What happened, while freighted with racial significance, was actually conditioned by class conflicts within white society. Once established, the "peculiar institution" would have consequences for centuries to come. During the nineteenth century, the political storm over slavery almost destroyed the nation. Since the Civil War and emancipation, race has continued to be largely defined in relation to African Americans—segregation, civil rights, the underclass, and affirmative action. Constituting the largest minority group in our society, they have been at the cutting edge of the Civil Rights Movement. Indeed, their struggle has been a constant reminder of America's moral vision as a country committed to the principle of liberty. Martin Luther King clearly understood this truth when he wrote from a jail cell: "We will reach the goal of freedom in Birmingham and all over the nation because the goal of America is freedom. Abused and scorned though we may be, our destiny is tied up with America's destiny."

Asian Americans have been here for over one hundred and fifty years, before many European immigrant groups. But as "strangers" coming from a "different shore," they have been stereotyped as "heathen," exotic, and unassimilable. Seeking "Gold Mountain," the Chinese arrived first, and what happened to them influenced the reception of the Japanese, Koreans, Filipinos, and Asian Indians as well as the Southeast Asian refugees like the Vietnamese and the Hmong. The 1882 Chinese Exclusion Act was the first law that prohibited the entry of immigrants on the basis of nationality. The Chinese condemned this restriction as racist and tyrannical. "They call us 'Chink,'" complained a Chinese immigrant, cursing the "white demons." "They think we no good! America cuts us off. No more come now, too bad!" This precedent later provided a basis for the restriction of European immigrant groups such as Italians, Russians, Poles, and Greeks. The Japanese painfully discovered that their accomplishments in America did not lead to acceptance, for during World War II, unlike Italian Americans and German Americans, they were placed in internment camps. Two-thirds of them were citizens by birth. . . . Today, Asian Americans represent the fastest-growing ethnic group. They have also become the focus of much mass media attention as "the Model Minority" not only for blacks and Chicanos, but also for whites on welfare and even middle-class whites experiencing economic difficulties.

Chicanos represent the largest group among the Hispanic population, which is projected to outnumber African Americans. They have been in the United States for a long time, initially incorporated by the war against Mexico. The treaty had moved the border between the two countries, and the people of "occupied" Mexico suddenly found themselves "foreigners" in their "native land.". . . The Chicano experience has been unique, for most of them have lived close to their homeland—a proximity that has helped reinforce their language, identity, and culture. This migration to El Norte has continued to the present. Los Angeles has more people of Mexican origin than any other city in the world, except Mexico City. A mostly mestizo people of Indian as well as African and Spanish ancestries, Chicanos currently represent the largest minority group in the Southwest, where they have been visibly transforming culture and society.

The Irish came here in greater numbers than most immigrant groups. Their history has been tied to America's past from the very beginning. Ireland represented the earliest English frontier: the conquest of Ireland occurred before the colonization of America, and the Irish were the first group that the English called "savages." In this context, the Irish past foreshadowed the Indian future. During the nineteenth century, the Irish, like the Chinese, were victims of British colonialism. While the Chinese fled from the ravages of the Opium Wars, the Irish were pushed from their homeland by "English tyranny." Here they became construction workers and factory operatives as well as the "maids" of America. Representing a Catholic group seeking to settle in a fiercely Protestant society, the Irish immigrants were targets of American nativist hostility. . . . The Irish came about the same time as the Chinese, but they had a distinct advantage: the Naturalization Law of 1790 had reserved citizenship for "whites" only. Their compatible complexion allowed them to assimilate by blending into American society. In making their journey successfully into the mainstream, however, these immigrants from Erin pursued an Irish "ethnic" strategy: they promoted "Irish" solidarity in order to gain political power and also to dominate the skilled blue-collar occupations, often at the expense of the Chinese and blacks. . . .

By looking at these groups from a multicultural perspective, we can comparatively analyze their experiences in order to develop an understanding of their differences and similarities. Race, we will see, has been a social construction that has historically set apart racial minorities from European immigrant groups. . . . A broad comparative focus also allows us to see how the varied experiences of different racial and ethnic groups occurred within shared contexts.

During the nineteenth century, for example, the Market Revolution employed Irish immigrant laborers in New England factories as it expanded cotton fields worked by enslaved blacks across Indian lands toward Mexico. Like blacks, the Irish newcomers were stereotyped as "savages," ruled by passions rather than "civilized" virtues such as self-control and hard work. The Irish saw themselves as the "slaves" of British oppressors, and during a visit to Ireland in the 1840s, Frederick Douglass found that the "wailing notes" of the Irish ballads reminded him of the "wild notes" of slave songs. The United States annexation of California, while incorporating Mexicans, led to trade with Asia and the migration of "strangers" from Pacific shores. In 1870, Chinese immigrant laborers were transported to Massachusetts as scabs to break an Irish immigrant strike; in response, the Irish recognized the need for interethnic working-class solidarity and tried to organize a Chinese lodge of the Knights of St. Crispin. After the Civil War, Mississippi planters recruited Chinese immigrants to discipline the newly freed blacks. During the debate over an immigration exclusion bill in 1882, a senator asked: If Indians could be located on reservations, why not the Chinese?

Other instances of our connectedness abound. In 1903, Mexican and Japanese farm laborers went on strike together in California: their union officers had names like Yamaguchi and Lizarras, and strike meetings were conducted in Japanese and Spanish. The Mexican strikers declared that they were standing in solidarity with their "Japanese brothers" because the two groups had toiled together in the fields and were now fighting together for a fair wage. . . . During the 1920s, elite universities like Harvard worried about the increasing numbers of Jewish students, and new admissions criteria were instituted to curb their enrollment. Jewish students were scorned for their studiousness and criticized for their "clannishness.". . .

The signs of America's ethnic diversity can be discerned across the continent—Ellis Island, Angel Island, Chinatown, Harlem, South Boston, the Lower East Side, places with Spanish names like Los Angeles and San Antonio or Indian names like Massachusetts and Iowa. Much of what is familiar in America's cultural landscape actually has ethnic origins. The Bing cherry was developed by an early Chinese immigrant named Ah Bing. American Indians were cultivating corn, tomatoes, and tobacco long before the arrival of Columbus. The term *okay* was derived from the Choctaw word *oke,* meaning "it is so." There is evidence indicating that the name *Yankee* came from Indian terms for the English—from *eankke* in Cherokee and *Yankwis* in Delaware. Jazz and blues as well as rock and roll have African-American origins. The "Forty-Niners" of the Gold Rush learned mining techniques from the Mexicans; American cowboys acquired herding skills from Mexican *vaqueros* and adopted their range terms—such as *lariat* from *la reata, lasso* from *lazo,* and *stampede* from *estampida.*

Songs like "God Bless America," "Easter Parade," and "White Christmas" were written by a Russian-Jewish immigrant named Israel Baline, more popularly known as Irving Berlin.

Furthermore, many diverse ethnic groups have contributed to the building of the American economy, forming what Walt Whitman saluted as "a vast, surging, hopeful army of workers." They worked in the South's cotton fields, New England's textile mills, Hawaii's canefields, New York's garment factories, California's orchards, Washington's salmon canneries, and Arizona's copper mines. . . .

In his recent study of Spain and the New World, *The Buried Mirror*, Carlos Fuentes points out that mirrors have been found in the tombs of ancient Mexico, placed there to guide the dead through the underworld. He also tells us about the legend of Quetzalcoatl, the Plumed Serpent: when this god was given a mirror by the Toltec deity Tezcatlipoca, he saw a man's face in the mirror and realized his own humanity. For us, the "mirror" of history can guide the living and also help us recognize who we have been and hence are. In *A Distant Mirror*, Barbara W. Tuchman finds "phenomenal parallels" between the "calamitous 14th century" of European society and our own era. We can, she observes, have "greater fellow-feeling for a distraught age" as we painfully recognize the "similar disarray," "collapsing assumptions," and "unusual discomfort."

But what is needed in our own perplexing times is not so much a "distant" mirror, as one that is "different." While the study of the past can provide collective self-knowledge, it often reflects the scholar's particular perspective or view of the world. What happens when historians leave out many of America's peoples? What happens, to borrow the words of feminist Adrienne Rich, "when someone with the authority of a teacher" describes our society, and "you are not in it"? Such an experience can be disorienting—"a moment of psychic disequilibrium, as if you looked into a mirror and saw nothing."

Through their narratives about their lives and circumstances, the people of America's diverse groups are able to see themselves and each other in our common past. . . . Much of America's past, they point out, has been riddled with racism. At the same time, these people offer hope, affirming the struggle for equality as a central theme in our country's history. At its conception, our nation was dedicated to the proposition of equality. What has given concreteness to this powerful national principle has been our coming together in the creation of a new society. . . .

Finally, how do we see our prospects for "working out" America's racial crisis? Do we see it as through a glass darkly? Do the televised images of racial hatred and violence that riveted us in 1992 during the days of rage in Los Angeles frame a future of divisive race relations . . . ? Or will Americans of diverse races and ethnicities be able to connect themselves to a larger narrative? Whatever happens, we can be certain that much of our society's future will be influenced by which "mirror" we choose to see ourselves. America does not belong to one race or one group, the people in this study remind us, and Americans have been constantly redefining their national identity from the moment of first contact on the Virginia shore. By sharing their stories, they invite us to see ourselves in a different mirror.

Mexican American Identity and Culture

Américo Paredes

Américo Paredes was a professor emeritus of English at the University of Texas at Austin and is considered a pioneer of Mexican American studies and American folklore. Paredes was one of the founders of the Center for Mexican American Studies and the Center for Intercultural Studies of Folklore and Ethnomusicology at the University of Texas. He received the Charles Fankel Prize from the National Endowment for the Humanities. His study of Mexican folk ballads, *With a Pistol in His Hand*, represents a major contribution to the disciplines of anthropology, history, and folklore. In this essay, Paredes analyzes the changing nature of culture and identity along the United States border with Mexico. He also examines the relationship between Mexican American folklore and the development of ethnic identity.

Conflict—cultural, economic, and physical—has been a way of life along the border between Mexico and the United States, and it is in the so-called Nueces–Río Grande strip where its patterns were first established. Problems of identity also are common to border dwellers, and these problems were first confronted by people of Mexican culture as a result of the Texas revolution. For these reasons, the Lower Río Grande area also can claim to be the source of the more typical elements of what we call the culture of the border. . . .

The culture of the border is not only historically dynamic but has its regional variations as well. Because it is difficult to generalize on so vast an area, this essay focuses on one region, the northeast. It sometimes is referred to as the Lower Río Grande Border or simply, the Lower Border. In a strictly chronological sense, this region may claim priority over the other areas. If we view a border not simply as a line on a map but, more fundamentally, as a sensitized area where two cultures or two political systems come face to face, then the first "border" between English-speaking people from the United States and people of Mexican culture was in the eastern part of what is now the state of Texas. And this border developed even before such polit-

Excerpted from Américo Paredes, "The Problem of Identity in a Changing Culture: Popular Expressions of Culture Conflict Along the Lower Rio Grande Border," in *View Across the Border: The United States and Mexico*, edited by Stanley R. Ross. Reprinted with permission from the author.

ical entities as the Republic of Mexico and the Republic of Texas came into being. Its location shifted as the relentless drive south and west . . . pushed a hotly contested borderline first to the Nueces and later to the Río Grande.

Certain folklore themes and patterns spread from the Nueces–Río Grande area to other parts of the border as cultural conflict spread. That a distinctive border culture spread from the Nueces–Río Grande area to other border regions (as well as to other areas of the West) is a thesis explored by Professor Walter Prescott Webb in *The Great Plains*. In the chapter "The Cattle Kingdom," Webb sees his "kingdom" as developing a peculiar "civilization." This "cattle culture" was the result of a union of northern Mexican ranchero culture, including techniques of raising cattle and horses, with new technological improvements brought in by Anglo Americans, especially such things as revolvers, barbed wire, and lawyers versed in the intricacies of land titles.

Much has been written about the blending of cultures in the southwestern United States, though less has been said about the impact of United States culture on northern Mexico. The number of books written about the influence of Mexican (or Spanish) architecture in the southwestern United States, if placed one beside another, would fill an extremely long bookshelf. Even more has been said and written about Mexican foods in the United States, an interest also manifest in the number of "Mexican" restaurants in almost any American town or city, patronized for the most part by WASP [white Anglo-Saxon Protestant] Americans. The ultimate in Mexican food in the Southwest and other areas are the quick-service chains that now sell tacos the way other chains sell hamburgers and hot dogs.

"Mexican food" is of course defined as tamales, tacos, enchiladas, chalupas, nachos, tostadas, frijoles refritos, and delicacies of that sort. What is rarely noted is that for the border Mexican of the past couple of centuries these foods have been almost as exotic as they are to the WASP American. One of the popular etymologies given for "greaser," an epithet applied by Anglo Americans to Mexicans, is that the term arose when the Anglos first encountered Mexicans in the Nueces–Río Grande area and were struck by the greasiness of Mexican food. O. Henry has enshrined this stereotype in his poem "Tamales," according to which "Don José Calderón Santos Espirition Vicente Camillo Quintana de Ríos de Rosa y Ribera" takes revenge on the Texans for having killed his grandfather at San Jacinto by selling greasy tamales to Anglos:

> What boots it if we killed
> Only one greaser,
> Don José Calderón?
> This is your deep revenge,
> You have greased all of us,
> Greased a whole nation
> With your Tamales . . .

The author of "The Little Adobe Casa," a parody of "The Little Sod Shanty on My Claim," has a much better idea of the border Mexican's fare, perhaps based on more direct experience than O. Henry's. The singer lives in Mexico, where "the Greaser roams about the place all day." Still, he keeps hoping that some "dark eye mujer" will consent to be his wife. Meanwhile,

> My bill of fare is always just the same
> Frijoles and tortillas
> Stirred up in chili sauce
> In my little adobe casa on the plains.

Frijoles, chiles, and tortillas were the standard fare along the border, as everywhere else in Mexico, except that the tortillas were more likely to be made of flour than of *nixtamal* [cooked maize], while the frijoles were never refried but boiled and mashed into a soupy stew— *caldudos.* Tamales were eaten once a year, at Christmas after the yearly hog was killed; and a taco was any snack made of a rolled tortilla with some kind of filling. For a more varied daily menu there might be rice with chicken or dried shrimp, beef either fresh or dried, as well as almost any other part of the steer. And for a real treat there was *cabrito* [goatmeat].

Bigfoot (El Patón) Wallace, who was captured by Mexican troops . . . , used his alleged sufferings in captivity as an excuse for the barbarities he committed against Mexican civilians . . . during the Mexican War. One of the examples of his mistreatment at Mexican hands is mentioned in John Duval's romanticized biography of Wallace. Wallace complained that after being captured, and during the time he spent along the Río Grande, all he ever was given to eat were beans, tortillas, and roast goatmeat. Nowadays, many of Wallace's fellow countrymen journey all the way from central Texas to "in" eating spots on the Río Grande, to satisfy their craving for beans, tortillas, and roast goatmeat. But perhaps Bigfoot found border Mexican food too greaseless for his taste; he probably missed his sidemeat and the rich gravies he was accustomed to sopping his biscuits in.

A better case for the blending of Anglo-American culture with that of the northern Mexican ranchero may be made in respect to the more practical elements of the "cattle culture." Cattle and horses, as well as land, were Mexican to begin with; and when the Anglo took them over he also adopted many of the techniques developed by the ranchero for the handling of stock. The vocabulary related to the occupation of the vaquero also became part of the blend. These things also have merited the attention of scholars and popular writers alike, especially those interested in the process whereby the rough Mexican ranchero was transformed into the highly romanticized American cowboy. All these subjects, from food and architecture to the birth of the cowboy, have attracted interest mainly from the viewpoint of their impact on the culture of the United States. My own interest in the cowboy has been a bit more intercultural, I believe, and it has focused on the manner in which an ideal pattern of male behavior has been developed interculturally along the border, subsequently to influence the male self-image first in the United States and later in Mexico. I refer to the familiar figure of popular fiction and popular song—the mounted man with his pistol in hand. Take the Mexican ranchero, a man on horseback par excellence, add the six-chambered revolver, and you have the American cowboy of fiction and popular legend—the ideal figure of many an Anglo male. The cowboy as a *macho* image was carried by the Texan, along with other elements of the "cattle culture," to other areas of the border, as well as to other parts of the West. The idea of the cowboy as the American *macho* becomes so pervasive that it can influence the private and public life of Theodore Roosevelt, as well as the scholarly writings of historians like Walter Prescott Webb. Finally—aided in the last stages of the process by such books as Webb's *The Texas Rangers*—the cowboy has his apotheosis in Hollywood. The impact on a people of an idea or an ideal may be gauged by its influence on the folksongs of that people. Thus, it is worth noting that by 1910 the work of John A. Lomax, the great collector of North American folksongs, was beginning to make Americans see the cowboy as the national image and find the essence of the North American spirit in the cowboy, as expressed in the cowboy's songs. At that time the Mexican Revolution was just getting under way, and it would be almost a generation before romantic nationalists in Mexico would discover the essence of *mexicanismo* in the *corridos* [popular ballads] of the Revolution.

The cowboy had influenced the border Mexican long before, and in a very direct way, because "cowboy" began as the name of the Anglo cattle thieves who raided the Nueces–Río Grande area in the late 1830s, and who, revolver in hand, began the dispossession of the Mexican on the north bank of the Río Grande. Understandably, the border Mexican developed a fascination for the revolver as a very direct symbol of power; he had learned the power of the pistol the hard way. Mexicans lent the image of the vaquero to their neighbors to the north, and the image returned to Mexico wearing a six-shooter and a Stetson hat. The cowboy *macho* image influenced the Revolution, . . . but it was after the Revolution that the cycle was completed, with the singing *charros* of the Mexican movies. And it was at about this same time that anthropologists and psychoanalysts discovered *machismo* in Mexico and labeled it as a peculiarly Mexican way of behavior.

But life along the border was not always a matter of conflicting cultures; there was often cooperation of a sort, between ordinary people of both cultures, since life had to be lived as an everyday affair. People most often cooperated in circumventing the excessive regulation of ordinary intercourse across the border. In other words, they regularly were engaged in smuggling. Smuggling, of course, has been a common activity wherever Mexicans and North Americans have come in contact; and this goes back to times long before Mexico's independence, when Yankee vessels used to make periodic smuggling visits to the more out-of-the-way Mexican ports. The famous Santa Fe Trail, begun about 1820 between Santa Fe and Independence, Missouri, may be considered one of the largest and most publicized smuggling operations in history. But even earlier, smuggling had been fairly general from the United States into Texas. The fact that the United States had consumer goods to sell and that Mexicans wanted to buy made smuggling inevitable, and many otherwise respected figures in the early history of the Southwest seem to have indulged in the practice. Smuggling could even be seen in those early days as a kind of libertarian practice, a protest against the harsh customs laws of the colonial times that throttled Mexico's economy. So, smuggling was not peculiar to the Nueces–Río Grande area, while the romanticizing of the smuggler as a leader in social protest was not limited even to the border areas as a whole. One has only to remember Luis Inclán's *Astucia,* where tobacco smugglers in interior Mexico are idealized as social reformers of the gun and hangman's noose. (It is worth mentioning, however, that Inclán's hero sends to the United States for *pistolas giratorias* [revolving pistols] to accomplish his pre–Porfirio Díaz [president of Mexico] version of iron-fisted law and order.) . . .

The Treaty of Guadalupe Hidalgo settled the conflict over territory between Mexico and the United States, officially at least. It also created a Mexican-American minority in the United States, as has often been noted. But it did not immediately create a border situation all along the international line. The *nuevomejicano* in Santa Fe, the *californio* in Los Angeles, and the *tejano* in San Antonio were swallowed whole into the North American political body. The new border—an imaginary and ill-defined line—was many miles to the south of them, in the uninhabited areas that already had separated them from the rest of Mexico before the war with the United States. The immediate change in customs demanded of *tejanos, californios,* and *nuevomejicanos* was from that of regional subcultures of Mexico to occupied territories within the United States.

Such was not the case with the people of the Lower Río Grande. A very well-defined geographic feature—the Río Grande itself—became the international line. And it was a line that cut right through the middle of what had once been Nuevo Santander. The river, once a focus of regional life, became a symbol of separation. The kind of borderline that separates ethnically related peoples is common enough in some parts of Europe; but in the earliest stages of the border between Mexico and the United States, it was typical only of the Lower Río Grande, with some exceptions such as the El Paso area. Here a pattern was set that would later become typical of the whole border between Mexico and the United States. Irredentist movements were shared with other occupied areas such as New Mexico, though the Cortina and Pizaña uprisings of 1859 and 1915 respectively were strongly influenced by the proximity of the international boundary. More to our point was the general flouting of customs and immigration laws, not so much as a form of social or ethnic protest but as part of the way of life.

When the Río Grande became a border, friends and relatives who had been near neighbors—within shouting distance across a few hundred feet of water—now were legally in different countries. If they wanted to visit each other, the law required that they travel many miles up or down stream, to the nearest official crossing place, instead of swimming or boating directly across as they used to do before. It goes without saying that they paid little attention to the requirements of the law. When they went visiting, they crossed at the most convenient spot on the river; and, as is ancient custom when one goes visiting loved ones, they took gifts with them: farm products from Mexico to Texas, textiles and other manufactured goods from Texas to Mexico. Legally, of course, this was smuggling, differing from contraband for profit in volume only. Such a pattern is familiar to anyone who knows the border, for it still operates, not only along the Lower Río Grande now but all along the boundary line between Mexico and the United States.

Unofficial crossings also disregarded immigration laws. Children born on one side of the river would be baptized on the other side, and thus appear on church registers as citizens of the other country. This bothered no one since people on both sides of the river thought of themselves as *mexicanos,* but United States officials were concerned about it. People would come across to visit relatives and stay long periods of time, and perhaps move inland in search of work. After 1890, the movement in search of work was preponderantly from Mexico deep into Texas and beyond. The ease with which the river could be crossed and the hospitality of relatives and friends on either side also was a boon to men who got in trouble with the law. It was not necessary to flee over trackless wastes, with the law hot on one's trail. All it took was a few moments in the water, and one was out of reach of his pursuers and in the hands of friends. If illegal crossings in search of work were mainly in a northerly direction, crossings to escape the law were for the most part from north to south. By far, not all the Mexicans fleeing American law were criminals in an ordinary sense. Many were victims of cultural conflict, men who had reacted violently to assaults on their human dignity or their economic rights.

Resulting from the partition of the Lower Río Grande communities was a set of folk attitudes that would in time become general along the United States-Mexican border. There was a generally favorable disposition toward the individual who disregarded customs and immigration laws, especially the laws of the United States. The professional smuggler was not a figure of reproach, whether he was engaged in smuggling American woven goods into Mexico or Mexican tequila into Texas. In folklore there was a tendency to idealize the smuggler, especially the *tequilero* [tequila smuggler], as a variant of the hero of cultural conflict. The smuggler, the illegal alien looking for work, and the border-conflict hero became identified with each other in the popular mind. They came into conflict with the same American laws and sometimes with the same individual officers of the law, who were all looked upon as *rinches*—a border-Spanish rendering of "ranger." Men who were Texas Rangers, for example, during the revenge killings of Mexicans after the Pizaña uprising of 1915 later were border patrolmen who engaged in gun-battles with *tequileros*. So stereotyped did the figure of the *rinche* become that Lower Río Grande Border versions of "La persecución de Villa" ["The Persecution of Pancho Villa"] identify [General John] Pershing's soldiers as *rinches*.

A *corrido* tradition of intercultural conflict developed along the Río Grande, in which the hero defends his rights and those of other Mexicans against the *rinches*. The first hero of these *corridos* is Juan Nepomuceno Cortina, who is celebrated in an 1859 *corrido* precisely because he helps a fellow Mexican.

> Ese general Cortina
> es libre y muy soberano,
> han subido sus honores
> porque salvo a un mexicano.

> That general Cortina is quite sovereign and free;
> The honor due him is greater, for he saved a Mexican's life.

Other major *corrido* heroes are Gregorio Cortez (1901), who kills two Texas sheriffs after one of them shoots his brother; Jacinto Treviño (1911), who kills several Americans to avenge his brother's death; Rito García (1885), who shoots several officers who invade his home without a warrant; and Aniceto Pizaña and his *sediciosos* [seditious group] (1915). Some *corrido* heroes escape across the border into Mexico; others, like Gregorio Cortez and Rito García, are betrayed and captured. They go to prison but they have stood up for what is right. As the "Corrido de Rito García" says,

> . . . me voy a la penitencia
> por defender mi derecho.

> I am going to the penitentiary because
> I defended my rights.

The men who smuggled tequila into the United States during the twenties and early thirties were no apostles of civil rights, nor did the border people think of them as such. But in his activities, the *tequilero* risked his life against the old enemy, the *rinche*. And, as has been noted, smuggling had long been part of the border way of life. Still sung today is "El corrido de Mariano Reséndez" about a prominent smuggler of textiles into Mexico, circa 1900. So highly respected were Reséndez and his activities that he was known as "El Contrabandista." Reséndez, of course, violated Mexican laws; and his battles were with Mexican customs officers. The *tequilero* and his activities, however, took on an intercultural dimension; and they became a kind of coda to the *corridos* of border conflict.

The heavy-handed and often brutal manner that Anglo lawmen have used in their dealings with border Mexicans helped make almost any man outside the law a sympathetic figure, with the *rinche* or Texas Ranger as the symbol of police brutality. . . . The border Mexican's tolerance of smuggling does not seem to extend to traffic in drugs. The few *corridos* that have been current on the subject . . . take a negative view of the dope peddler. Yet Carrasco's death in 1976 at the Huntsville (Texas) prison, along with two women hostages, inspired close to a dozen *corridos* with echoes of the old style. The sensational character of Carrasco's death cannot be discounted, but note should also be taken of the unproved though widely circulated charges that Carrasco was "executed" by a Texas Ranger, who allegedly shot him through the head at close range where Carrasco lay wounded. This is a scenario familiar to many a piece of folk literature about cultural conflict—*corridos* and prose narratives—the *rinche* finishing off the wounded Mexican with a bullet through the head. It is interesting to compare the following stanzas, the first from one of the Carrasco *corridos* and the other two from a *tequilero* ballad of the thirties.

El capitán de los rinches
fue el primero que cayó
pero el chaleco de malla
las balas no traspasó.

The captain of the Rangers was the first one to fall.
But the armored vest he was wearing did not let the bullets through.

En fin de tanto invitarle
Leandro los acompañó;
en las lomas de Almiramba
fue el primero que cayo.

They kept asking him to go, until Leandro went with them;
In the hills of Almiramba, he was the first one to fall.

El capitán de los rinches
a Silvano se acercó,
y en unos cuantos segundos
Silvano García murió.

The captain of the Rangers came up close to Silvano;
And in a few seconds Silvano García was dead.

Similar attitudes are expressed on the Sonora-Arizona border, for example, when the hard-case hero of "El corrido de Cananea" is made to say,

Me agarraron los cherifes
al estilo americano,
como al hombre de delito,
todos con pistola en mano.

The sheriffs caught me, in the American style,
As they would a wanted man, all of them pistol in hand.

The partition of Nuevo Santander was also to have political effects, arising from the strong feeling among the Lower Río Grande people that the land on both sides of the river was equally theirs. This involved feelings on a very local and personal level, rather than the rhetoric of national politics, and is an attitude occasionally exhibited by some old Río Grande people to this day. Driving north along one of today's highways toward San Antonio, Austin, or Houston, they are likely to say as the highway crosses the Nueces, "We are now entering Texas." Said in jest, of course, but the jest has its point. Unlike Mexicans in California, New Mexico, and the old colony of Texas, the Río Grande people experienced the dismemberment of Mexico in a very immediate way. So the attitude developed, early and naturally, that a border Mexican was *en su tierra* [in his native land] in Texas even if he had been born in Tamaulipas. Such feelings, of course, were the basis for the revolts of Cortina and Pizaña. They reinforced the borderer's disregard of political and social boundaries. And they lead in a direct line to the Chicano movement. . . . For the Chicano does not base his claim to the Southwest on royal land grants or on a lineage that goes back to the Spanish conquistadores. On the contrary, he is more likely to be the child or grandchild of immigrants. He bases his claim to Aztlan on his Mexican culture and his mestizo heritage.

Conversely, the Texas-born Mexican continued to think of Mexico as "our land" also. That this at times led to problems of identity is seen in the folksongs of the border. In 1885, for example, Rito García protests illegal police entry into his home by shooting a few officers of Cameron County, Texas. He makes it across the river and feels safe, unaware that Porfirio Díaz has an extradition agreement with the United States. Arrested and returned to Texas, according to the *corrido*, he expresses amazement,

Yo nunca hubiera creído
que mi país tirano fuera,
que Mainero me entregara
a la nación extranjera

I never would have thought that my country would be so
unjust,
That Mainero would hand me over to a foreign nation.

And he adds bitterly,

Mexicanos, no hay que fiar
en nuestra propia nación,
nunca a vayan a buscar
a México protección.

Mexicans, we can put no trust in our own nation;
Never go to Mexico asking for protection.

But the *mexicanos* to whom he gives this advice are Texas Mexicans.

An even more interesting case dates back to 1867, the year [Mexican emperor] Maximilian surrendered at Querétaro. A few days before this event, on May 5, Mexicans celebrated another event just as historic, the fifth anniversary of the defeat of the French at Puebla by Mexican troops under Ignacio Zaragoza. The little town of San Ignacio, on the Texas side of the river, celebrated the Cinco de Mayo with a big festival at which a local *guitarrero* [guitarist] sang two of his songs, especially composed for the occasion. One was "A Zaragoza," in praise of the victor over the French at Puebla; the other was "A Grant," in praise of Ulysses S. Grant, the victor over the Confederacy. The same set of symbols—flag, honor, country—is used in both songs.

PERSONAL IDENTITY AND ETHNICITY

Mary C. Waters

Mary C. Waters is a professor of sociology at Harvard University and is the author of *Ethnic Options: Choosing Identities in America*, which focuses on second-, third-, and fourth-generation European immigrants in the United States. She suggests that a sense of ethnicity among these groups continues to form a significant aspect of their self-identity. In this selection, Waters describes ethnicity as an evolving, changing concept that individuals may incorporate into their sense of self.

Census and survey data on later-generation white ethnics in the 1970s and 1980s have yielded an interesting and what may appear at first to be a startling finding—ethnic identity is a social process that is in flux for some proportion of the population. Far from being an automatic labeling of a primordial characteristic, ethnic identification is, in fact, a dynamic and complex social phenomenon. . . .

The degree of intermarriage and geographic and social mobility among whites of European extraction in the United States means that they enjoy a great deal of choice and numerous options when it comes to ethnic identification. This population can increasingly choose how much and which parts of their ethnicity to make a part of their lives. Yet for the most part these options or choices are not recognized as such by the people who enjoy them.

The idea that ethnic self-identification is not biological or primordial and that it involves a great deal of choice may be startling to some people, because it is counterintuitive when viewed from the popular conception of ethnicity. The widely held societal definitions of race and ethnicity take the categories and classifications in place at any one time for granted, and hence do not generally see them as socially created or dynamic in nature. The common view among Americans is that ethnicity is primordial, a personal, inherited characteristic like hair color. Most people assume that ethnic groups are stable categories and that one is a member of a particular ethnic group because one's ancestors were members of that group. Thus one is French because one's ancestors were French and because the category French exists and has meaning. One may know that the Normans, the

Excerpted from Mary Waters, *Ethnic Options: Choosing Identities in America*. Reprinted with permission from the University of California Press.

Franks, the Burgundians, and the Gauls were once separate groups who came to be known as French, but that does not necessarily make the category French any less "real" to a particular individual.

Yet most sociologists study ethnicity from social, situational, or rational points of view, seeking to understand the forces in society that create, shape, and sustain ethnic identity. They often defend such approaches from an opposite, biologically based understanding of ethnicity. Sociologists' definitions of ethnicity stress that it involves the *belief* on the part of people that they are descended from a common ancestor and that they are part of a larger grouping. The idea that membership in an ethnic group need not be hereditary, or directly related to a common lineage, is a direct challenge to this widely held view. . . .

People's *belief* that racial or ethnic categories are biological, fixed attributes of individuals does have an influence on their ethnic identities. This popular understanding of ethnicity means that people behave as if it were an objective fact even when their own ethnicity is highly symbolic. This belief that ethnicity is biologically based acts as a constraint on the ethnic choices of some Americans, but there is nonetheless a range of latitude available in deciding how to identify oneself and whether to do so in ethnic terms. Whites enjoy a great deal of freedom in these choices; those defined in "racial" terms as non-whites much less.

Black Americans, for example, are highly socially constrained to identify as blacks, without other options available to them, even when they believe or know that their forebears included many non-blacks. Up until the mid twentieth century, many state governments had specific laws defining one as black if one-quarter or more of one's ancestry was black, or one out of four of one's grandparents were. As late as the 1970s the Current Population Survey required its interviewers to determine the race of those they were interviewing "by observation." As a result some people were classified as "Negro" by the interviewer who did not classify themselves that way: 1.9 million out of a total of 22.9 million who were classified as "Negro" by the interviewer answered something else for themselves. Most answered "Don't Know" or "Other"; 126,000 said they were Spanish. In any case, this shows how some groups may be socially constrained to accept an ethnic identity. The assumption by the official census takers was that others could determine the race of an individual on "objective," quasi-biological grounds without that person necessarily agreeing. There were no such assumptions or actual legal definitions governing choice of ancestry or identity for white Americans.

The fact that there are no longer any *legal* constraints on choice of ancestry does not mean these choices are completely "free" of social control. Certain ancestries take precedence over others in the societal rules on descent and ancestry reckoning. If one believes one is part

English and part German and identifies in a survey as German, one is not in danger of being accused of trying to "pass" as non-English and of being "redefined" English by the interviewer. But if one were part African and part German, one's self-identification as German would be highly suspect and probably not accepted if one "looked" black according to the prevailing social norms.

For white ethnics, however, ethnic identification involves *both* choice and constraint. Children learn both the basic facts of their family history and origins and the cultural content and practices associated with their ethnicity in their households. This process itself often involves a sifting and simplifying of various options.

One constructs an ethnic identification using knowledge about ancestries in one's background. Such information generally comes from family members and/or some type of formal documentation, such as a family Bible or a will. This information is selectively used in the social construction of ethnic identification within the prevailing historical, structural, and personal constraints. Often people know that their ancestors are from many different backgrounds, yet for one reason or another they identify with only some, or in some cases none, of their ancestors.

The interaction between choice and constraint in ethnic identification is most obvious in the case of the children of mixed marriages. But even the relationship between believed ethnic origin and self-identification for people of single ancestry involves a series of choices. For instance, individuals who believe their ancestry to be solidly the same in both parents' backgrounds can (and often do) choose to suppress that ancestry and self-identify as "American" or try to pass as having an ancestry they would like to have. The option of identifying as ethnic therefore exists for all white Americans, and further choice of *which* ethnicity to choose is available to some of them.

Furthermore, an individual's self-identification does not necessarily have to be the same at all times and places, although it can be. Someone whose mother is half Greek and half Polish and whose father is Welsh may self-identify as Greek to close friends and family and as Polish at work, or as Welsh on census documents. An individual may change ethnic identification over time, for various reasons. At various times and places, one is more or less at ease dropping or inventing a self-identification. In a local situation where everyone knows one's believed ethnic origins—for example, a small town where everyone knows your mother and father—it would be more difficult to self-identify exclusively with one or the other. If one moved to another locality this would probably become easier.

Beyond Racial-Identity Politics

Manning Marable

Manning Marable is a professor of African American studies at Columbia University and the author of the classic study of race and class in the United States: *How Capitalism Underdeveloped Black America*. This selection examines how race and ethnicity continue to affect the lives of all Americans. Marable discusses the ways in which race and ethnicity have been defined within society and the consequences of such definitions. The author clarifies some of the major problems in the construction of racial categories as fixed and permanent statuses.

Americans are arguably the most "race-conscious" people on earth. Even in South Africa, the masters of apartheid recognized the necessity to distinguish between "coloureds" and "black Africans." Under the bizarre regulations of apartheid, a visiting delegation of Japanese corporate executives or the diplomatic corps of a client African regime such as Malawi could be classified as "honorary whites." But in the US, "nationality" has been closely linked historically to the categories and hierarchy of national racial identity. Despite the orthodox cultural ideology of the so-called "melting pot," power, privilege and the ownership of productive resources and property has always been unequally allocated in a social hierarchy stratified by class, gender and race. Those who benefit directly from these institutional arrangements have historically been defined as "white," overwhelmingly upper class and male. And it is precisely here, within this structure of power and privilege, that "national identity" in the context of mass political culture is located. To be an "all-American" is, by definition, *not* to be an Asian-American, Pacific-American, American Indian, Latino, Arab-American or African-American. Or, viewed another way, the hegemonic ideology of "whiteness" is absolutely central in rationalising and justifying the gross inequalities of race, gender, and class experienced by millions of Americans relegated to the politically peripheral status of "Others.". . . "Whiteness" becomes the very "centre" for the dominant criteria for national prestige, decision-making, authority and intellectual leadership.

Ironically, because of the centrality of "whiteness" within the dom-

Excerpted from Manning Marable, "Beyond Racial Identity Politics: Towards a Liberation Theory for Multicultural Democracy," in *Race, Class, and Gender: An Anthology*, 2nd ed., edited by Margaret L. Anderson. Reprinted with permission from The Institute of Race Relations.

inant national identity, Americans generally make few distinctions between "ethnicity" and "race," and the two concepts are usually used interchangeably. Both the oppressors and those who are oppressed are, therefore, imprisoned by the closed dialectic of race. "Black" and "white" are usually viewed as fixed, permanent and often antagonistic social categories. Yet, in reality, "race" should be understood not as an entity, within the histories of all human societies, or grounded to some inescapable or permanent biological or genetic differences between human beings. "Race" is, first and foremost, an unequal relationship between social aggregates, characterised by dominant and subordinate forms of social interaction, and reinforced by the intricate patterns of public discourse, power, ownership and privilege within the economic, social and political institutions of society.

Race only becomes "real" as a social force when individuals or groups behave towards each other in ways which either reflect or perpetuate the hegemonic ideology of subordination and the patterns of inequality in daily life. These are, in turn, justified and explained by assumed differences in physical and biological characteristics, or in theories of cultural deprivation or intellectual inferiority. Thus, far from being static or fixed, race as an oppressive concept within social relations is fluid and ever changing. What is an oppressed "racial group" changes over time, geographical space and historical conjuncture. What is termed "black," "Hispanic" or "Oriental" by those in power to describe one human being's "racial background" in a particular setting can have little historical or practical meaning within another social formation which is also racially stratified, but in a different manner.

Since so many Americans view the world through the prism of permanent racial categories, it is difficult to convey the idea that radically different ethnic groups may have a roughly identical "racial identity" imposed on them. For example, although native-born African-Americans, Trinidadians, Haitians, Nigerians and Afro-Brazilians would all be termed "black" on the streets of New York City, they have remarkably little in common in terms of language, culture, ethnic traditions, rituals and religious affiliations. Yet they are all "black" racially, in the sense that they will share many of the pitfalls and prejudices built into the institutional arrangements of the established social order for those defined as "black." Similarly, an even wider spectrum of divergent ethnic groups—from Japanese-Americans, Chinese-Americans, Filipino-Americans and Korean-Americans to Hawaiians, Pakistanis, Vietnamese, Arabs and Uzbekis—are described and defined by the dominant society as "Asians" or, worse yet, as "Orientals." In the rigid, racially stratified American social order, the specific nationality, ethnicity and culture of a person of colour has traditionally been secondary to an individual's "racial category," a label of inequality which is imposed from without rather than constructed by the group from within. . . . The waves of recent immigrants create new concepts of what the older ethnic communities have been. The observations and generalisations we imparted "to racial identities" in the past no longer make that much sense.

In the United States, "race" for the oppressed has also come to mean an identity of survival, victimisation and opposition to those racial groups or elites which exercise power and privilege. What we are looking at here is *not* an *ethnic* identification or culture, but an awareness of shared experience, suffering and struggles against the barriers of racial division. These collective experiences, survival tales and grievances form the basis of an historical consciousness, a group's recognition of what it has witnessed and what it can anticipate in the near future. This second distinct sense of racial identity is both imposed on the oppressed and yet represents a reconstructed critical memory of the character of the group's collective ordeals. Both definitions of "race" and "racial identity" give character and substance to the movements for power and influence among people of colour.

CHAPTER 3

SEARCHING FOR THE AMERICAN DREAM

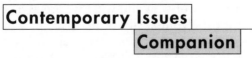

Contemporary Issues Companion

RACE MATTERS

Cornel West

Cornel West, a professor of African American studies at Harvard University and author of numerous award-winning books on race and American culture, examines the continued importance of race in American society. West stresses that race relations in the United States will continue to represent a pressing social issue, and he calls for a continued commitment to improving intergroup relations. Through such efforts, and with the leadership of informed political leaders, West believes that race relations in the United States will improve in the coming years.

What happened in Los Angeles in April of 1992 was neither a race riot nor a class rebellion. Rather, this monumental upheaval was a multiracial, trans-class, and largely male display of justified social rage. For all its ugly, xenophobic resentment, its air of adolescent carnival, and its downright barbaric behavior, it signified the sense of powerlessness in American society. Glib attempts to reduce its meaning to the pathologies of the black underclass, the criminal actions of hoodlums, or the political revolt of the oppressed urban masses miss the mark. Of those arrested, only 36 percent were black, more than a third had full-time jobs, and most claimed to shun political affiliation. What we witnessed in Los Angeles was the consequence of a lethal linkage of economic decline, cultural decay, and political lethargy in American life. Race was the visible catalyst, not the underlying cause.

The meaning of the earthshaking events in Los Angeles is difficult to grasp because most of us remain trapped in the narrow framework of the dominant liberal and conservative views of race in America, which with its worn-out vocabulary leaves us intellectually debilitated, morally disempowered, and personally depressed. The astonishing disappearance of the event from public dialogue is testimony to just how painful and distressing a serious engagement with race is. Our truncated public discussions of race suppress the best of who and what we are as a people because they fail to confront the complexity of the issue in a candid and critical manner. The predictable pitting of liberals against conservatives, Great Society Democrats against self-help Republicans, reinforces intellectual parochialism and political paralysis.

The liberal notion that more government programs can solve racial problems is simplistic—precisely because it focuses *solely* on the economic dimension. And the conservative idea that what is needed is a change in the moral behavior of poor black urban dwellers (especially poor black men, who, they say, should stay married, support their children, and stop committing so much crime) highlights immoral actions while ignoring public responsibility for the immoral circumstances that haunt our fellow citizens. . . .

To engage in a serious discussion of race in America, we must begin not with the problems of black people but with the flaws of American society—flaws rooted in historic inequalities and longstanding cultural stereotypes. How we set up the terms for discussing racial issues shapes our perception and response to these issues. As long as black people are viewed as a "them," the burden falls on blacks to do all the "cultural" and "moral" work necessary for healthy race relations. The implication is that only certain Americans can define what it means to be American—and the rest must simply "fit in.". . .

To establish a new framework, we need to begin with a frank acknowledgment of the basic humanness and Americanness of each of us. And we must acknowledge that as a people—*E Pluribus Unum*—we are on a slippery slope toward economic strife, social turmoil, and cultural chaos. If we go down, we go down together. The Los Angeles upheaval forced us to see not only that we are not connected in ways we would like to be but also, in a more profound sense, that this failure to connect binds us even more tightly together. The paradox of race in America is that our common destiny is more pronounced and imperiled precisely when our divisions are deeper. The Civil War and its legacy speak loudly here. And our divisions are growing deeper. Today, eighty-six percent of white suburban Americans live in neighborhoods that are less than 1 percent black, meaning that the prospects for the country depend largely on how its cities fare in the hands of a suburban electorate. There is no escape from our interracial interdependence, yet enforced racial hierarchy dooms us as a nation to collective paranoia and hysteria—the unmaking of any democratic order.

The verdict in the Rodney King case which sparked the incidents in Los Angeles was perceived to be wrong by the vast majority of Americans. But whites have often failed to acknowledge the widespread mistreatment of black people, especially black men, by law enforcement agencies, which helped ignite the spark. The verdict was merely the occasion for deep-seated rage to come to the surface. This rage is fed by the "silent" depression ravaging the country—in which real weekly wages of all American workers since 1973 have declined nearly 20 percent, while at the same time wealth has been upwardly distributed.

The exodus of stable industrial jobs from urban centers to cheaper labor markets here and abroad, housing policies that have created "chocolate cities and vanilla suburbs" (to use the popular musical artist George Clinton's memorable phrase), white fear of black crime, and the urban influx of poor Spanish-speaking and Asian immigrants—all have helped erode the tax base of American cities just as the federal government has cut its supports and programs. The result is unemployment, hunger, homelessness, and sickness for millions.

And a pervasive spiritual impoverishment grows. The collapse of meaning in life—the eclipse of hope and absence of love of self and others, the breakdown of family and neighborhood bonds—leads to the social deracination and cultural denudement of urban dwellers, especially children. We have created rootless, dangling people with little link to the supportive networks—family, friends, school—that sustain some sense of purpose in life. We have witnessed the collapse of the spiritual communities that in the past helped Americans face despair, disease, and death and that transmit through the generations dignity and decency, excellence and elegance. . . .

What is to be done? How do we capture a new spirit and vision to meet the challenges of the post-industrial city, post-modern culture, and post-party politics?

First, we must admit that the most valuable sources for help, hope, and power consist of ourselves and our common history. As in the ages of [Abraham] Lincoln, [Franklin D.] Roosevelt, and [Martin Luther] King, we must look to new frameworks and languages to understand our multilayered crisis and overcome our deep malaise.

Second, we must focus our attention on the public square—the common good that undergirds our national and global destinies. The vitality of any public square ultimately depends on how much we *care* about the quality of our lives together. The neglect of our public infrastructure, for example—our water and sewage systems, bridges, tunnels, highways, subways, and streets—reflects not only our myopic economic policies, which impede productivity, but also the low priority we place on our common life.

The tragic plight of our children clearly reveals our deep disregard for public well-being. About one out of every five children in this country lives in poverty, including one out of every two black children and two out of every five Hispanic children. Most of our children— neglected by overburdened parents and bombarded by the market values of profit-hungry corporations—are ill-equipped to live lives of spiritual and cultural quality. Faced with these facts, how do we expect ever to constitute a vibrant society?

One essential step is some form of large-scale public intervention to ensure access to basic social goods—housing, food, health care, education, child care, and jobs. We must invigorate the common good with a mixture of government, business, and labor that does not follow any existing blueprint. After a period in which the private sphere has been sacralized and the public square gutted, the temptation is to make a fetish of the public square. We need to resist such dogmatic swings.

Last, the major challenge is to meet the need to generate new leadership. The paucity of courageous leaders—so apparent in the response to the events in Los Angeles—requires that we look beyond the same elites and voices that recycle the older frameworks. We need leaders—neither saints nor sparkling television personalities—who can situate themselves within a larger historical narrative of this country and our world, who can grasp the complex dynamics of our peoplehood and imagine a future grounded in the best of our past, yet who are attuned to the frightening obstacles that now perplex us. Our ideals of freedom, democracy, and equality must be invoked to invigorate all of us, especially the landless, propertyless, and luckless. Only a visionary leadership that can motivate "the better angels of our nature," as Lincoln said, and activate possibilities for a freer, more efficient, and stable America—only that leadership deserves cultivation and support.

This new leadership must be grounded in grass-roots organizing that highlights democratic accountability. Whoever *our* leaders will be . . . , their challenge will be to help Americans determine whether a genuine multiracial democracy can be created and sustained in an era of global economy and a moment of xenophobic frenzy.

Let us hope and pray that the vast intelligence, imagination, humor, and courage of Americans will not fail us. Either we learn a new language of empathy and compassion, or the fire this time will consume us all.

Women's Achievement: The Impact of Race and Gender

Maxine Baca Zinn and Bonnie Thornton Dill

Maxine Baca Zinn, a professor of sociology at Michigan State University, and Bonnie Thornton Dill, a professor of women's studies at the University of Maryland, are experts in the area of race, ethnicity, gender, and class and how these factors impact such groups as Mexican American and African American women. Zinn and Dill outline the major sources of inequality that confront women of color. They suggest that conditions in the labor market are largely responsible for inequality and discuss a variety of the ways in which women have struggled to reduce such inequalities.

People of color, both men and women, have encountered severe economic and social dislocations from the time of their arrival in the United States until the present. In colonial America, American Indians faced war, disease, and a deliberate program of extermination. Africans died in large numbers in the "middle passage," the journey that brought them from their native continent to enslavement in the United States. Mexicans were incorporated into the United States as the result of a war and, along with Asian workers who were forced to live and work in "bachelor" communities far from their homes and families, died in large numbers working to build the mines and railroads. Up through the present, these groups have experienced periods of severe animosity marked by lynchings, race riots, and other forms of public violence.

Today, women of color on average receive the lowest wages, hold the worst jobs, and are more likely to be unemployed. They have the highest rates of infant mortality and births out of wedlock. They are also more likely to live in poverty and to be single mothers than their White counterparts.

Women of color are subordinated in this way because patterns of hierarchy, domination, and oppression based on race, class, gender, and sexual orientation are built into the structure of our society.

Inequality, in other words, is structural or socially patterned. Too often explanations of these inequalities suggest that biology or culture is key. We argue, however, that biological traits, such as race and gender, are relevant only because they are socially ranked and rewarded. It is the *social* response to these biological characteristics that results in inequality. Though we do not discount the importance of culture, the problem with cultural differences as the primary explanation of inequality is the tendency to marginalize each cultural group, to view it as unique, and to imply that each differs from some presumed standard. This often leads to blaming a people's cultural values and practices for their subordination.

An image that helps convey how social structure limits opportunity and represents the relationship between structure and culture is found in Gloria Naylor's novel *The Women of Brewster Place*. The characters in this story live on a dead-end street that has been closed off by a brick wall. The wall separates Brewster Place from the rest of the community. It shuts out light to apartments, it creates a dark and unprotected area where destructive activities occur, and its presence suggests that there is only one way out. The wall on Brewster Place is a powerful symbol of the ways racial oppression, sexual exploitation, and class domination constrain the life chances and choices of the women who live there. . . .

Labor arrangements are at the core of race and gender inequalities. Social location in the labor market means that opportunities are influenced by *who* people are—by their being male or female; White, Black, Latina, American Indian, or Asian; rich or poor—rather than what their skills and abilities are. . . .

Social Agency: Confronting the "Walls"

Race, class, and gender create a matrix of domination that women of color "experience (and resist) on three levels, namely the level of personal biography, the group level of the cultural context created by race, class and gender, and the systemic level of social institutions.". . .

In addition to the formal limits of social structure, women of color have also been subjected to cultural assaults. Cultural assaults are systematic attacks on the institutions and forms of social organization that are fundamental to the maintenance and flourishing of a group's culture. They are a way dominant groups control and manage subordinate groups of people. They range from legal prohibitions against the use of drums among African slaves, and against the immigration of the wives of Chinese men, to informal practices that denigrate the cultural patterns of these groups while elevating the values and practices of the dominant groups.

In spite of these obstacles, women of color have shaped their lives and those of their families through acts of quiet dignity and steadfast determination. Their actions have included revolt and rebellion, creative conflict and social change, adaptation and accommodation.

The involvement of women in slave rebellions, American Indian wars, labor revolts in the fields and mines of the West and Southwest, and contemporary urban uprisings is well documented. As the primary laborers in families, kinship networks, and communities, women have also been engaged in more subtle forms of resistance. In their families and communities, many worked to create new institutions and to help their children maintain an autonomous cultural identity—a vision of self in society based on their own distinctive culture, separate from the ideals and images that the dominant culture sought to impose upon them. . . .

Rethinking Gender

Social location is a complex (and often contradictory) determinant of women's distinctive experiences. For example, Patricia Hill Collins, in *Black Feminist Thought* (1990), argues that "a self-defined, articulated Black feminist standpoint" exists and that it has been the source of Black women's ability to resist the controlling images of the dominant society, which depicted them as mammies, matriarchs, whores, welfare recipients, and unwed mothers. This standpoint provided alternative images that encouraged them to fight to change the world in which they and their children lived. . . . Images and ideologies about women of color are used not only to control them but also to rationalize their subordinate position in the society.

Grounding gender studies in women's differences can reveal relations that remain obscure from other vantage points. Starting with women of color can lead, for example, to what Collins (1990) calls the "matrix of domination," an analysis that raises questions about the primacy of gender as an analytic category. . . . By looking at social context along the way, we discover that within a social order that is racially formed and class based, the categories "women" and "men" do not exist as broad universals, although there are women and men in particular historically located relations. . . . Many women of color are oppressed not only by race, class, and gender but by systems that privilege heterosexuality. The discriminations that lesbians of color face occur within this matrix of domination. . . .

Diversity, in other words, reveals how genders are constructed out of interlocking systems of inequality. The lives of women of color are not a variation of a more general model of American womanhood. Instead, their experiences are formed by many of the same forces that shape the lives of others. In given historical moments, those forces combine to create differences among women. . . .

Once we acknowledge that all women are affected by the racial order of society, we gain "new starting points for feminist thought and action.". . . Growing primarily out of the experiences of racial-ethnic women, which are themselves varied, multiracial feminism does not offer a singular or unified feminism but a body of knowledge situating women and men in multiple systems of domination. Nevertheless, it treats racial inequality as a vital shaper of women's and men's lives and advances a coherent and powerful premise—that racial ancestry, ethnic heritage, and economic status are as important as gender for analyzing the social construction of women and men.

GOOD NEWS ABOUT BLACK AMERICA

Ellis Cose

Newsweek journalist Ellis Cose discusses the changing realities in Black America: crime is down, unemployment is down, and incomes are rising. Black Americans are beginning to rethink their opportunities, perspectives, and goals. Most of all, white Americans are accepting the accomplishments of African Americans. Cose recognizes that problems continue to exist but points out that change seems to be taking place, often at an accelerated pace.

It was a stunning vision of racial equality, manifested in a simple yet stirring mantra: "I have a dream." Though Martin Luther King Jr.'s cherished utopia has not arrived, it seems considerably less remote than it did in August 1963 when, from the Washington Mall, King challenged America to make his dream come true. African-Americans are no longer relegated, as he lamented, to "a lonely island of poverty" in the midst of plenty. By a wide array of measures, now is a great time—the best time ever—to be black in America.

Black employment and home ownership are up. Murders and other violent crimes are down. Reading and math proficiency are climbing. Out-of-wedlock births are at their lowest rate [since the 1950s]. Fewer blacks are on welfare than at any point in recent memory. More are in college than at any point in history. And the percentage of black families living below the poverty line is the lowest it has been since the Census Bureau began keeping separate black poverty statistics in 1967. Even for some of the most persistently unfortunate—uneducated black men between 16 and 24—jobs are opening up, according to a [1999] study of hard-luck cases in 322 urban areas by researchers at Harvard University and the College of William and Mary.

More and more blacks have entered the realm of the privileged and have offices in (or tantalizingly near to) the corridors of corporate and political power. Some control multimillion-dollar budgets and reside in luxurious gated communities. They are, by any criteria, living large—walking testaments to the transformative power, to the possibility, of America.

"I really think there is a new phenomenon out there," says Eddie Williams, head of the Joint Center for Political and Economic Studies,

Reprinted from Ellis Cose, "Good News About Black America," *Newsweek*, June 7, 1999. Reprinted with permission.

the nation's premier think tank on blacks and politics. According to the center, the number of black elected officials has nearly sextupled since 1970, and [as of 1999] stands at roughly 9,000. In a poll late [in 1998] by the Joint Center, blacks were more likely than whites—for the first time in the history of this survey—to say they were better off financially than in the previous year (51 percent compared with 31.5 percent). A new *Newsweek* Poll confirms that the finding is not a fluke. Seventy-one percent of blacks (compared with 59 percent of whites) told *Newsweek's* pollsters that they expected their family incomes to rise during the next 10 years. Fifty-seven percent of blacks (compared with 48 percent of whites) foresaw better job opportunities ahead. As Los Angeles gangbanger turned music entrepreneur Darrin Butler, 28, sums it up, "From where I'm sitting, everything is looking bright."

This sunniness is reflected in the country's popular imagination, which freely celebrates the appeal and accomplishments of African-Americans. Michael Jordan, Lauryn Hill, Colin Powell—pick your icon; if you are touched at all by American culture your idol is likely to be black. There have always been black successes and superstar achievers, but never before has black been quite so beautiful to so many admirers of every hue. "When did you ever think you would see black men as the heroes of white children?" asks Bobby William Austin, head of the Village Foundation, an Alexandria, Va.-based non-profit that runs programs for young black men.

Today's upswing in black fortune is unfolding in a singular context, against the backdrop of a superheated economy that has been booming since April 1991. That expansion, the longest ever in a time of peace, has been a boon to Americans of every race. It would be a mistake, however, to credit the economy alone for the sense of hope sprouting in many black communities. Even as the strong economy has made bigger dreams possible, a strong resurgence of black self-confidence and self-determination has made their realization more probable. Indeed, blacks polled by *Newsweek* credited black churches (46 percent) and black self-help (41 percent) for the upturn in black conditions. It would also be a mistake to assume that today's good times have brought good tidings to all blacks. They have not. More black men than ever languish in prisons. Black academic achievement still lags that of whites. And suicides among young black men have risen sharply, reflecting a deep "sense of hopelessness," says Jewelle Taylor Gibbs, a psychologist and University of California, Berkeley, professor. And fear is pervasive that an economic downturn—or the legal-political assault on affirmative action—could wipe out blacks' tenuous gains.

Nonetheless, for a community yet haunted by the memory of Jim Crow, this is a remarkable moment. One of the most dramatic signs of progress is the explosion of productive activity as once desolate inner-city neighborhoods, such as Chicago's North Lawndale, come to life.

In 1966, this area on Chicago's West Side was so blighted that Martin Luther King rented an apartment there to call attention to it. Then things got worse. The area was largely incinerated by the riots that broke out in the wake of King's assassination in 1968. More than half of the population moved out between 1960 and 1990. Now new construction is shooting up. Homes are selling for as much as $275,000 apiece. And the young black professionals flocking back to buy them talk of renaissance and hope reborn.

"People wrote this area off. They didn't believe middle-class African-Americans would come back here. Now we're making this neighborhood work," says Demetrius Barbee. For Barbee, a Blockbuster executive, and her husband, Gerald, a medical-equipment technician, trading in a fancy North Lake Shore Drive address for a North Lawndale dream house was not merely a matter of getting good quality for a good price. It was an investment of hope in the very idea of a community coming back from the dead.

Homan Square, the development where the Barbees now live, resulted from a serendipitous confluence of events. Sears, having moved its onetime world headquarters out of the area, had plenty of well-maintained land it was willing to donate to the project. Mayor Richard M. Daley was eager to facilitate—providing, among other assistance, grants to first-time homeowners. And an important developer, the Shaw Co., saw the value of the enterprise. The Homan Square experiment in urban reclamation has covered six city blocks with 299 units of housing, 133 of them owner-occupied single-family homes. It has also spawned a health clinic, several new businesses and numerous other construction projects. Perhaps most important, it has inspired other developers. Just southeast of Homan Square sits a new shopping center anchored by a Dominick's supermarket and a 10-screen Cineplex Odeon Theater. A few blocks away, another town-house development has gone up. Central City Productions, a local black-owned entertainment company, plans to build a $150 million, 337,000-square-foot television-studio complex. And other projects are pending.

Though few urban ghettos have seen a turnaround as promising as North Lawndale's, withered communities elsewhere are rebounding as well. In the Elmhurst area of Oakland, Calif., new buildings are rising from the rubble. Unlike in Chicago, where a major company took the lead, this turnaround effort—like others in New York, Chattanooga, Tenn., Savannah, Ga., and elsewhere—is community based. In the past year alone Allen Temple Baptist Church has generated more than $20 million worth of new construction projects. The church plans to open a 60,500-square-foot Family Living Center . . . (with activities for everyone from children to senior citizens) and has broken ground for a 24-unit complex for AIDS/HIV patients.

"This is a congregation that long ago decided to take matters into its own hands," says Doris Britt, a church member and director of admissions at UC Berkeley's School of Social Welfare. Longtime congregant Joe Villa traces the can-do attitude to the late '70s. As white homeowners and white-owned businesses and banks took flight, the church kept the faith. Determined to provide a place for community residents to bank, "we contacted the National Credit Union Administration and figured out how to charter our own credit union," recalls Villa, who became its volunteer president. That credit union (which primarily serves church members) will be 20 years old next year and now holds more than $10 million in assets—making it the largest African-American church credit union in the country. Community-based activists are not only initiating urban-renewal projects, but driving down teenage births and crime all over America, contends Angela Blackwell, founder of Policy Link, an Oakland-based research and advocacy organization. "Poor people just got sick of it," she says. Others give more credit to government policies, including tough anticrime measures and welfare reform. Kerman Maddox, chairman of the political-science department at Los Angeles Southwest College, in South-Central L.A., says his female students are taking school more seriously and are less likely to have babies. "In the past, I'd say half my 18- to 22-year-old students had kids," says Maddox. "The number has dropped dramatically." He believes welfare-reform provisions "that no longer reward them for having more kids" are the principal reason.

Whatever the motivations (and they are necessarily multiple), more young people are moving to take control of their lives; and the result seems to be a better shot at success. As Shykiesha Walker, the 17-year-old president of the Young Girls Keeping it Real Club, in Watts, puts it, "We're just trying to keep ourselves out of trouble, achieve a higher goal in life."

Across the country, Piney Woods Life School, a private boarding academy in rural Mississippi, is stoking that hunger for success. Started at the turn of the century to educate children of Mississippi field hands, it has evolved into a haven for mistreated or troubled black kids from across America. Many come from backgrounds similar to Kenyatah's, a 16-year-old junior whose parents, both junkies, kicked her out of their Washington, D.C., home at the age of 4. She ended up with relatives, also addicts, and spent time living on the street. Serendipity and a recommendation from a friend of her aunt brought Kenyatah to Piney Woods, and she is grateful for the change. "Where I'm from, you don't learn anything [in school]," she says.

At Piney Woods academics are stressed, and self-pity is not an option. Over the last several years, ACT scores for Piney Woods seniors have risen from an average of 9.8 to an average of 18.1—compared with a national average of 22. "We've set a goal of having our young people exceed the national average on the ACT within the next three years," says school president Charles Beady Jr. Piney Woods graduates routinely go on to Ivy League colleges. Many also become ambassadors of deliverance, spreading the word that black children can triumph, no matter how or where their lives begin.

The significant reversal of black fortunes is a signal event, one that "must be acknowledged and celebrated," says Joe Hicks, executive director of the Los Angeles Human Relations Commission. Yet, for the most part, blacks are not celebrating it, which raises an inevitable question: if the news in black America is so good these days, why are people not dancing in the streets? Why are civil-rights leaders not proclaiming it from the rooftops? Why has the dialogue on racial relations not fundamentally changed to accentuate the progress instead of the lingering problems?

Ward Connerly, the controversial black businessman and driving force behind Proposition 209, the ballot measure that eliminated affirmative action in California state government, thinks the reason has a lot to do with the fossilized attitude of many blacks—particularly those in the leadership class. Even though society has transformed itself, says Connerly, many African-Americans are "locked into that mind-set of the '60s that society is racist. . . . We just can't let go. Our leaders . . . can't let go. I won't say they have a vested interest in maintaining the status quo, although I think that's a possibility." Harvard sociologist Orlando Patterson agrees. In the aftermath of the civil-rights revolution, "blaming racism" made good politics and fashionable social science, he says. That era is ending, in Patterson's view, "but, tragically, Afro-American leaders now seem trapped by the fire they started."

In African-American leadership circles, Patterson's indictment strikes a nerve. It even evokes limited agreement. Yvonne Scruggs-Leftwich, executive director of the Black Leadership Forum, an umbrella group of civil-rights organizations, concedes, "We don't often enough acknowledge where there have been successes." Nonetheless, civil-rights leaders resent and reject the view that they are a bunch of self-serving doomsayers. "We *have* celebrated the economy, the reduction in unemployment, the reduction in teen-pregnancy rates," says Hugh Price, head of the National Urban League.

The problem is that although certain blacks are thriving, others are not. Many of those "beneath the surface of socioeconomic viability," as sociologist Elijah Anderson describes them, are worse off than ever. Many blighted, black neighborhoods lack the equivalent of a Homan Square or an Allen Temple and are dying slow, painful deaths. And in that fact lies a leadership challenge and a philosophical dilemma. How can civil-rights leaders acknowledge the real and evident progress without encouraging complacency? How can they keep the pressure on to "move the glass from half-full to three-quarters full," in Price's words, if they give up the language of crisis and damnation? How do they avoid playing into the hands of those who would eliminate affirmative action, voting-rights enforcement and so many other things that are largely responsible for the black progress on display today? "To the extent you proclaim your success, other people forget about you," worries the Joint Center's Eddie Williams.

Then there is the fear—one deeply felt not only among the black leadership class but among much of the black general population—that the good times may be transient. What happens, skeptics ask, when the economy hits bottom? Or if the attacks on affirmative action ultimately eliminate opportunities, only recently won, in both the private and the public sectors?

In addition, there is this cold reality: for every upbeat statistic that engenders joy, there is a dismal number—or a skeptical reading—that invites alarm. And there are millions of personal experiences that conflict with the rosy statistics. In 1998, the jobless rate for blacks 20 to 24 years old was 16.8 percent, down from 24.5 percent in 1985; but that means little to Travon Netherly, a student at L.A. Southwest College. Recently, says Travon, four of his brothers applied for a job at an Orange County amusement park. Despite the help-wanted ad in the window, all were turned away. "My brothers were willing to take anything, even wear one of those Snoopy costumes," says Netherly, who bitterly adds, "It don't take skills to be Snoopy."

LATIN USA

Brook Larmer

By the year 2020 Hispanics will be the largest ethnic group in the United States. Hispanics are changing the face of America both culturally and politically. In this essay, Brook Larmer, a journalist for *Newsweek*, explains that Hispanics are retaining their Latino identity and still becoming American as they infuse new types of music, cuisine, literature, and art into the American landscape. The driving force behind the Hispanicization of America is what this *Newsweek* article calls "Generation Ñ." This generation consists of such national figures as singers Gloria Estefan and Ricky Martin and many others who are becoming successful Latino Americans.

Strolling along northwest Eighth Street in Miami—a.k.a. Calle Ocho—is like taking a trip through another country. But . . . the sights and sounds of Calle Ocho were both intensely foreign and undeniably American. A crowd of angry Cuban exiles marched down the street denouncing the U.S. Coast Guard's use of force to round up six Cuban refugees near a local beach the day before. From the sidelines, other Latinos looked on: prim Honduran clerks at an evangelical bookstore, spiffed-up businessmen at an Argentine steakhouse, sweaty construction workers eating Salvadoran *pupusas*. Merengue music blasted indifferently from the Do-Re-Mi music shop. But the elderly Cubans playing dominoes in Maximo Gomez Park stood and joined in with the protesters: "Libertad! Libertad!"

Could this be the face of America's future? Better believe it. No place in the United States is quite so international as Miami; even the Latinos who run the city joke that they like it "because it's so close to America." But Miami, like New York and Los Angeles, is ground zero for a demographic upheaval that is unfolding across America. Like the arrival of European immigrants at the turn of the century, the tide of Hispanic immigrants—and the fast growth of Latino families—has injected a new energy into the nation's cities.

Latinos are changing the way the country looks, feels and thinks, eats, dances and votes. From teeming immigrant meccas to small-town America, they are filling churches, building businesses and cele-

Reprinted from Brook Larmer, "Latin USA," *Newsweek*, June 12, 1999. Reprinted with permission.

brating their Latin heritage. In a special *Newsweek* Poll of Latinos, 83 percent said being Hispanic was important to their identity. They are overwhelmingly Roman Catholic; 42 percent go to church once a week. They've become a potent, increasingly unpredictable political force: 37 percent of 18- to 34-year-old Latinos say they are independent, about twice as many as their Hispanic elders. In America, a country that constantly redefines itself, the rise of Latinos also raises questions about race, identity and culture—and whether the United States will ever truly be one nation.

The numbers couldn't be clearer. Fueled by massive (and mostly legal) immigration and high birthrates, the Latino population has grown 38 percent since 1990—to 31 million—while the overall population has grown just 9 percent. And with more than a third of the Latino population still under 18, the boom is just beginning. By the year 2005, Latinos are projected to be the largest minority in the country, passing non-Hispanic blacks for the first time. By 2050, nearly one quarter of the population will be Latino. "The [African-American] civil-rights slogan was 'We shall overcome'," says Christy Haubegger, the 30-year-old founding editor of the bilingual magazine *Latina*. "Ours is going to be 'We shall overwhelm'."

They may just have the muscle to back that up—particularly in politics. Though they accounted for only 6 percent of those who voted in the 1998 midterm elections, Hispanics are clustered in 11 key states, with a total of 217 out of the 270 Electoral College votes needed for the presidency. And neither party has a lock on this new force. "Latinos are the soccer moms of the year 2000," says Gregory Rodriguez of the New America Foundation. Is it any wonder that Al Gore and George W. Bush were both on campaign stops in Florida and California . . . , eagerly greeting voters in Spanish?

The driving force behind the Latino wave are members of a cohort that is sometimes called Generation Ñ. These young Hispanics—the Latin Gen X—are influential not simply because of their huge numbers. They are making their mark—and making all things Latin suddenly seem cool. Jose Canseco, a 35-year-old Cuban-American, and Dominican-born Sammy Sosa, 30, lead the great American home-run derby. Ricky Martin, 27, and Jennifer Lopez, 28, top the pop-music charts. Actors Benjamin Bratt, 35, and Salma Hayek, 30, are quickening the national pulse.

Is the rest of America ready? Hip Anglos on both coasts are dancing salsa, learning Spanish and dabbling in Nuevo Latino cuisine. And every fifth grader seems to know the lyrics of "Livin' La Vida Loca." But many Latinos doubt whether America can easily move past the stereotypes that depict them as illegals, gangbangers or entertainers. "Don't try to understand Latinos through [Ricky Martin]," says Manuel Magaña, 21, a University of Michigan senior. "It's like trying to figure out Americans by listening to the Backstreet Boys."

Latinos can't be neatly pigeonholed. They come from 22 different countries of origin, including every hybrid possible. Many are white, some are black, but most are somewhere in between. Some Latino families have been in the United States for centuries, since the days when much of the Southwest was still a part of Mexico. Others, like the six Cuban refugees, [are new arrivals]. (The Coast Guard freed them a day later.) Many Latinos are assimilating into cycles of urban blight; 40 percent of Latino children now live in poverty, the highest rate ever. But millions of Hispanics are also moving into the middle class, speaking English, inter-marrying and spending cash—lots of it. U.S. Latinos pump $300 billion a year into the economy.

Not everybody has been eager to give Latinos a big *abrazo* [hug]. When California voters passed propositions limiting immigrant rights and Washington tightened federal immigration policy in the mid-1990s, Latinos took it as a call to arms. The best weapons of defense were citizenship and the vote. Between 1994 and 1998, Latino voting in nationwide midterm elections jumped 27 percent even as overall voter turnout dropped 13 percent. The 2000 presidential election may show even more dramatic increases: Latino leaders aim to register an additional 3 million voters by then.

Latinos have long leaned Democratic (Clinton got 72 percent), but their vote is alluring these days precisely because it is up for grabs— and Generation Ñ seems intent on keeping it that way. Gore edged out Bush among all Latinos polled, 29 percent to 28 percent, but Generation Ñ voters favored Bush by a margin of 9 percent. Nobody understands how Latinos can swing an election more than Nevada Sen. Harry Reid, a Democrat. During his tight 1998 race, Reid's friend, boxing promoter Bob Arum, persuaded Oscar De La Hoya to join the campaign. The charismatic boxer did two fund-raisers, a public rally and several Spanish media spots. "He's the reason I'm in the Senate now," says Reid. Don't believe him? The senator won by just 428 votes.

Latinos are flattered to be considered hot commodities, whether as voters, consumers, employees or entertainers. But their aspirations, and their importance to American society, run much deeper than mere social acceptance. They are not "crossing over" into mainstream America; they are already here, getting more influential by the day, so the rest of America must learn to adapt as well. "Something tremendous is happening," says 30-year-old novelist Ixta Maya Murray. "This generation of Latinos is going to change the way America looks at itself." On the last Independence Day of the millennium, a new nation is being born.

What Is to Be Done?: Creating an Equal Society

Orlando Patterson

Orlando Patterson, a professor of sociology at Harvard University and the author of the award-winning *Slavery and Social Death: A Comparative Study,* provides an overall assessment of the status of African Americans in the United States. Although surveys indicate a general improvement in the daily lives of African Americans, Patterson suggests that continued efforts are required to reduce the racial tensions and conflicts still present in American society. The author suggests several ways to ensure that all groups have access to the American dream.

The great majority of Afro-Americans—some 23 million persons making up more than 70 percent of the aggregate—have benefited from the enormous progress made by both Afro- and Euro-Americans over the past forty-five years in resolving the nation's "racial" crisis. They are a hardworking, disproportionately God-fearing, law-abiding group of people who share the same dreams as their fellow citizens, love and cherish the land of their birth with equal fervor, contribute to its cultural, military, and political glory and global triumph out of all proportion to their numbers, and, to every dispassionate observer, are, in their values, habits, ideals, and ways of living, among the most "American" of Americans. It is striking that, as of October 1995, some 67 percent of Afro-Americans said that they still believed in the American Dream, and Afro-Americans were only 2 percent less likely than Euro-Americans to say that they were farther away from attaining the American Dream than they had been ten years ago.

For this two-thirds of the Afro-American population, Martin Luther King Jr.'s dream has *not* been deferred, as so many Euro-American liberals and Afro-American advocates insultingly insist, misleading the world. . . .

A sound grasp of this remarkable achievement must be the starting point of any assessment of America's "racial" problem. There is still a serious problem: let that be clear. Failures, especially in the persistence of urban slums and the ethnic bias in incarceration, rightly outrage most Afro-Americans as well as caring Euro-Americans. But it is irresponsible, patronizing, and downright racist of analysts and reporters in academia, public life, and the media to persist in viewing all Afro-Americans as a single, homogeneous group of downtrodden outsiders, racked with chronic problems and constantly sour about their lot and their country. For those who find it hard to believe that there are any happy, contented Afro-American persons out there in America, let the facts speak for themselves. When the National Opinion Research Center of the University of Chicago asked a random sample of Afro-Americans the following question in 1994—"Taken all together, how would you say things are these days, would you say you are very happy, pretty happy, or not too happy?"—fully 78 percent of them said that they were either very happy or pretty happy.

This response was no fluke. A Gallup poll in June 1997 found equally high levels of satisfaction in most areas of life by Afro-Americans. Thus, 74 percent were satisfied with the way things were going in their personal lives, up from 55 percent in 1979; three-fourths were satisfied with their housing condition, up from 49 percent in 1973; 74 percent were satisfied with their present standard of living, up from 45 percent in 1973; and 73 percent were satisfied with their jobs, compared with 66 percent in 1973. While only 53 percent of Afro-Americans were satisfied with their household income, this was entirely explained in class terms. Their dissatisfaction is an accurate reflection of their relatively lower income and not any chronic ethnic unhappiness with their lot; once class is taken into account, the difference in levels of satisfaction with standard of living between Euro-Americans and Afro-Americans vanishes.

We Must Change the Way We Talk About and Interpret Our So-Called "Race" Problem

• One of the first things to be done is to change the language of intergroup relations. The term *race* itself must be abandoned. . . . We should, instead, talk about ethnic groups and relations—if we must—rather than racial groups and relations; and the distinction between "race" and ethnicity should be abandoned as meaningless and potentially dangerous. It is incredible that the United States Census Bureau still continues to ask Americans to classify themselves according to "race" in addition to ethnic ancestry. Quite apart from the absurdities into which this distinction has gotten the agency with respect to so-called Hispanics, it is pernicious that the nation's Census Bureau is perpetuating this relic of the Nazi era. The term *race* should be banished from the Census questionnaire immediately.

    • We should drop the terms *black* and *white* when talking about Afro-Americans and Euro-Americans. I find it hard to believe that the nation's writers do not shudder at the sheer infelicity of referring to someone as a "black" or a "white." Not only are the terms *black* and *white* denotatively loaded in favor of Euro-Americans—as a check in *The Oxford English Dictionary* will attest in lurid detail—but by their emphasis on the somatic, they reinforce and legitimize precisely that biological notion of "race" that we claim we want to be rid of.

The term *racist* is still a meaningful one, but should be used only to designate persons who believe in the existence of ranked, genetically separate "races" and who explain human behavioral differences primarily in genetic or somatic terms. These include academic racists such as Arthur Jensen, Charles Murray and Leonard Jeffries, politicians such as David Duke and Louis Farrakhan, and the declining minority of the U.S. population—presently about a fifth of the nation—who still hold to this execrable dogma.

• In most cases where supposed racism is at issue, the more appropriate charge is either ethnocentrism or class prejudice. All human beings are prejudiced, Afro-Americans no less than others. It is natural to discriminate and categorize. These qualities are fundamental to all thought and sensibility. Indeed, we actively cultivate many kinds of prejudices, such as our prejudices toward freedom, democracy, and altruism, and much of what we call education, especially in the arts and humanities, is simply the cultivation of our capacity to discriminate between good and evil, the beautiful and the coarse, and refinement and vulgarity.

Ethnocentrism is the hurtful misapplication of our capacity to categorize and discriminate to particular aggregates of persons, especially those that are self-identified as ethnic groups. It consists of two egregious errors, and it is very important that we recognize its twofold nature. One error is the stereotyping of ethnic *aggregates* with negative attributes: "Jews are clannish and deceptive"; "Italian-Americans are prone to organized crime"; "The Irish are drunkards who beat their wives"; "Poles are stupid"; "Afro-Americans are socially and intellectually inferior"; and so on. The second is the tendency to judge *individuals* entirely or primarily in terms of the stereotyped attributes of the groups with which they are identified: John Brown over there is stupid because he is an Afro-American; Sidney Weinstein next door cannot be trusted because he is Jewish.

I distinguish between these two related aspects of ethnocentrism because, contrary to what many analysts think, they do not necessarily go together, especially in America. It is possible to be prejudiced against a collectivity of persons, especially one that is self-identified as an ethnic group, without being prejudiced against individual members of that group. In other words, it is possible to be anti-Semitic, or to dislike Afro-Americans as a group, and yet treat individual Jews and Afro-Americans one encounters quite fairly. The sardonic expression "Some of my best friends are Jews, Afro-Americans, etc." is aimed precisely at this apparent contradiction. The nation's newspapers often present tragic cases of it: Afro-American and Euro-American youth who maim and kill persons from the other ethnic group in what are clearly "racially motivated" acts often turn out to have close personal friends from the group they have so viciously stereotyped. And every middle-class minority person knows of at least one or two supervisors in organizations who are scrupulously fair with minority persons even though they are known to be racists. . . . Many Euro-Americans, faced with an *individual* who is Afro-American, are likely to be supportive of that individual in, for example, his claim to government assistance, but "confronted with blacks *as a group,* a significant number of whites practice a racial double standard."

On the other hand, it is possible to be individually prejudiced in "racial" or ethnic terms without holding such prejudices about the ethnic group with which the person is identified. This may be so because the prejudiced individual, on principle, does not believe in attributing qualities to groups. Many conservatives, for example, simply reject the reality of groups over and beyond individuals and families. . . . Recent studies of the attitude of employers toward Afro-American inner-city youths reveal marked individualized ethnic prejudice toward them even in cases where we know that these employers are not prejudiced toward Afro-Americans in general. How do we know? Not simply because the employers all insist they are not group prejudiced, but, more tellingly, because a large proportion of Afro-American employers exhibit exactly similar prejudice toward these youths. These employers are often themselves prominent members of the local Afro-American community, and it is obviously absurd to claim that they are racists against their own self-identified ethnic group. What we have, instead, is the kind of prejudice that has come to be known by the awkward term *statistical discrimination.* Whatever we call it, it is a clear example of individualized ethnic prejudice in the absence of generalized group prejudice.

Both versions of ethnocentric prejudice are wrong and dangerous, and we have to work hard toward their elimination, but we must recognize that formidable barriers stand in the way. In a large, heterogeneous society like America it can sometimes be costly to always do the right thing and judge every person one meets solely on the basis of reliable, individualized information on them. If I find myself walking alone on a street near South Boston and I see a large, rednecked Euro-American with a bulbous nose and long dirty blond hair dressed in studded black leather lumbering toward me, I am going to take evasive action, however statistically prejudiced against working-class Irish-Americans I know such an act to be. I would react the same way if I saw a group of hooded Afro-American homeboys bopping down the street with stony-eyed stares. How we sanction this kind of prejudice will depend on the relative probabilities of injury to both individuals and the potential damage of such injuries. In what may be called the menacing youth situation, the probability of being injured, while small, is nonetheless nonnegligible.

We cannot assume that there is no probability of injury to the party avoided in this situation. Minority youth, especially Afro-Americans, often suffer hurt feelings as a result of such evasive action. Indeed, when the frequency of psychological injury in casual ethnic encounters and the actual statistics of victimization by strange youth are considered, it may well be true that the probability of injury is greater for the avoided person than it is for the avoider. The problem, however, is not simply a matter of the odds of injury, but of the nature of the costs incurred in the event that one guesses wrong. In the menacing youth situation, the costs run the gamut from verbal abuse to catastrophic physical injury for the person making the judgment call whether to trust or to take evasive action. For the avoided person there is no such range of injury, since it does not extend beyond a temporary sense of being slighted.

With an employer, however, the probabilities of injury and the range of such injuries are different. Employers have the resources to gain more information on people seeking employment, and while the cost of being rejected for work can be catastrophic for the job seeker, not to mention the inner-city communities from which he and the majority of similarly rejected youth come, they do not go beyond the costs of firing and rehiring for the employer. These should be viewed as the necessary costs of doing business in a heterogeneous society that for generations willfully and maliciously shut out the vast majority of a subpopulation from the discipline and culture of the industrial process solely on the basis of their appearance. What is more, in the long run the society of the employer who statistically discriminates ends up paying far more in taxes to maintain the unemployed and to correct the social problems they create. Such costs may not be acknowledged by the prejudiced employer for classic free-rider reasons. It is to solve this free-rider problem, and to make sure that employers do the right thing, that strictly enforced laws against discrimination in hiring are essential. The fact that Afro-American employers engage in this kind of prejudice is neither an excuse for it nor a reason for not strictly enforcing antidiscrimination laws. It does suggest, however, that this kind of discrimination is really a form of class prejudice rather than ethnic prejudice. Unfortunately, there are no laws against class prejudice, and it is unlikely that such laws will ever be passed or implemented.

Against the group version of ethnocentrism we should continue to educate young and old alike about the dangers of attributing negative stereotypes to particular groups or aggregates of people. Multicultural education's main claim for support is that, at its best, it attempts to do this. The main obstacle in the elimination of ethnic group prejudice, however, is the ironic fact of the very salience of ethnicity in American life and our commitment to the slippery ideal of ethnic pride.

Some have seriously questioned whether it is possible to promote ethnic diversity without inciting ethnic hostility and division. It can be done, as the case of Switzerland, with its French-, German-, and Italian-speaking subpopulations, attests, but it is difficult, and I am not sure whether the conditions that made the Swiss model possible hold in America. . . .

For the time being, I propose that we talk about ethnic rather than "racial" differences as the lesser of two evils, and that in our ethnic discourse we do everything to avoid negatively stereotyping other groups. Since the promotion of ethnic diversity encourages the celebration of positive stereotypes about other ethnic groups, and since most people find it hard to accept positive stereotypes without slipping into negative ones, we have our work cut out for us.

CHAPTER 4

PERSONAL REFLECTIONS ON RACE AND ETHNICITY

COLORED PEOPLE: A MEMOIR

Henry Louis Gates Jr.

Henry Louis Gates Jr. is a professor, the chair of the Department of African American Studies at Harvard University, and the author of numerous anthologies and books, including *Loose Canons: Notes on the Culture Wars*. In this introduction to his autobiography, he discusses the impact of race on his identity and on his interpersonal relationships with African Americans and individuals from diverse backgrounds. Gates's introduction is written as a letter to his daughters and he talks about his own sense of self as a mosaic in a multicultural American society. He suggests that, although his life is directly linked with African American communities, he sees himself as a product of many cultures.

Dear Maggie and Liza:

I have written to you because a world into which I was born, a world that nurtured and sustained me, has mysteriously disappeared. My darkest fear is that Piedmont, West Virginia, will cease to exist, if some executives on Park Avenue decide that it is more profitable to build a completely new paper mill elsewhere than to overhaul one a century old. Then they would close it, just as they did in Cumberland with Celanese, and Pittsburgh Plate Glass, and the Kelly-Springfield Tire Company. The town will die, but our people will not move. They will not *be* moved. Because for them, Piedmont—snuggled between the Allegheny Mountains and the Potomac River Valley—is life itself.

I have written to you because of the day when we were driving home and you asked your mother and me just exactly what the civil rights movement had been all about and I pointed to a motel on Route 2 and said that at one time I could not have stayed there. Your mother could have stayed there, but your mother couldn't have stayed there with me. And you kids looked at us like we were telling you the biggest lie you had ever heard. So I thought about writing to you.

I have written for another reason, as well. I remember that once we were walking in Washington, D.C., heading for the National Zoo, and you asked me if I had known the man to whom I had just spoken. I said no. And, Liza, you volunteered that you found it embarrassing that I would speak to a complete stranger on the street. It called to mind a trip I'd made to Pittsburgh with my father. On the way from his friend Mr. Ozzie Washington's sister's house, I heard Daddy speak to a colored man, then saw him tip his hat to the man's wife. (Daddy liked nice hats: Caterpillar hats for work, Dobbs hats for Sunday.) It's just something that you do, he said, when I asked him if he had known those people and why had he spoken to them.

Last summer, I sat at a sidewalk café in Italy, and three or four "black" Italians walked casually by, as well as a dozen or more blacker Africans. Each spoke to me; rather, each nodded his head slightly or acknowledged me by a glance, ever so subtly. When I was growing up, we always did this with each other, passing boats in a sea of white folk.

Yet there were certain Negroes who would avoid acknowledging you in this way in an integrated setting, especially if the two of you were the ones doing the integrating. Don't go over there with those white people if all you're going to do is Jim Crow yourselves—Daddy must have said that to me a thousand times. And by that I think he meant we shouldn't *cling* to each other out of habit or fear, or use protective coloration to evade the risks of living like any other human being, or use clannishness as a cop-out for exploring ourselves and possibly making new selves, forged in the crucible of integration. Your black ass, he'd laugh, is integrated already.

But there are other reasons that people distrust the reflex—the nod, the glance, the murmured greeting.

One reason is a resentment at being lumped together with thirty million African Americans whom you don't know and most of whom you will never know. Completely by the accident of racism, we have been bound together with people with whom we may or may not have something in common, just because we are "black." Thirty million Americans are black, and thirty million is a lot of people. One day you wonder: What do the misdeeds of a Mike Tyson have to do with me? So why do I feel implicated? And how can I not feel racial recrimination when I can feel racial pride?

Then, too, there were Negroes who were embarrassed about *being* Negroes, who didn't want to be bothered with race and with other black people. One of the more painful things about being colored was being colored in public around other colored people, who were embarrassed to be colored and embarrassed that we *both* were colored and in public together. As if to say: "Negro, will you *pul-lease* disappear so that I can get my own white people?" As if to say: "I'm not a Negro like other Negroes." As if to say: "I am a human being—let me be!"

For much of my adolescence and adulthood, I thought of these people as having betrayed the race. I used to walk up to them and call them *Brother* or *Sister,* loud and with a sardonic edge, when they looked like they were trying to "escape." When I went off to college, I would make the "conversion" of errant classmates a serious project, a political commitment.

I used to reserve my special scorn for those Negroes who were always being embarrassed by someone else in the race. Someone too dark, someone too "loud," someone too "wrong." Someone who dared to wear red in public. Loud and wrong: we used to say that about each other. Nigger is loud and wrong. "Loud" carried a triple meaning: speaking too loudly, dressing too loudly, and just *being* too loudly.

I do know that, when I was a boy, many Negroes would have been the first to censure other Negroes once they were admitted into all-white neighborhoods or schools or clubs. "An embarrassment to the race"—phrases of that sort were bandied about. Accordingly, many of us in our generation engaged in strange antics to flout those strictures. Like eating watermelon in public, eating it loudly and merrily, and spitting the seeds into the middle of the street, red juice running down the sides of our cheeks, collecting under our chins. Or taking the greatest pride in the Royal Kink. Uncle Harry used to say he didn't *like* watermelon, which I knew was a lie because I saw him wolf down slices when I was a little kid, before he went off to seminary at Boston University. But he came around, just like he came around to painting God and Jesus black, and all the seraphim and the cherubim, too. And I, from another direction, have gradually come around, also, and stopped trying to tell other Negroes how to be black.

Do you remember when your mother and I woke you up early on a Sunday morning, just to watch Nelson Mandela walk out of prison, and how it took a couple of hours for him to emerge, and how you both wanted to go back to bed and, then, to watch cartoons? And how we began to worry that something bad had happened to him on the way out, because the delay was so long? And when he finally walked out of that prison, how we were so excited and teary-eyed at Mandela's nobility, his princeliness, his straight back and unbowed head? I think I felt that there walked the Negro, as Pop might have said; there walked the whole of the African people, as regal as any king. And that feeling I had, that gooseflesh sense of identity that I felt at seeing Nelson Mandela, listening to Mahalia Jackson sing, watching Muhammad Ali fight, or hearing Martin Luther King speak, is part of what I mean by being colored. I realize the sentiment may not be logical, but I want to have my cake and eat it, too. Which is why I still nod or speak to black people on the streets and why it felt so good to be acknowledged by the Afro-Italians who passed my table at the café in Milan.

I want to be able to take special pride in a Jessye Norman aria, a Muhammad Ali shuffle, a Michael Jordan slam dunk, a Spike Lee movie, a Thurgood Marshall opinion, a Toni Morrison novel, James Brown's Camel Walk. Above all, I enjoy the unselfconscious moments of a shared cultural intimacy, whatever form they take, when no one else is watching, when no white people are around. Like Joe Louis's fights, which my father still talks about as part of the fixed repertoire of stories that texture our lives. You've seen his eyes shining as he describes how Louis hit Max Schmeling so many times and so hard, and how some reporter asked him, after the fight: "Joe, what would you have done if that last punch hadn't knocked Schmeling out?" And how ole Joe responded, without missing a beat: "I'da run around behind him to see what was holdin' him up!"

Even so, I rebel at the notion that I can't be part of other groups, that I can't construct identities through elective affinity, that race must be the most important thing about me. Is that what I want on my gravestone: Here lies an African American? So I'm divided. I want to be black, to know black, to luxuriate in whatever I might be calling blackness at any particular time—but to do so in order to come out the other side, to experience a humanity that is neither colorless nor reducible to color. Bach *and* James Brown. Sushi *and* fried catfish. Part of me admires those people who can say with a straight face that they have transcended any attachment to a particular community or group . . . but I always want to run around behind them to see what holds them up.

I am not Everynegro. I am not native to the great black metropolises: New York, Chicago, or Los Angeles, say. Nor can I claim to be a "citizen of the world." I am from and of a time and a place—Piedmont, West Virginia—and that's a world apart, a world of difference. So this is not a story of a race but a story of a village, a family, and its friends. And of a sort of segregated peace. What hurt me most about the glorious black awakening of the late sixties and early seventies is that we lost our sense of humor. Many of us thought that enlightened politics excluded it.

In your lifetimes, I suspect, you will go from being African Americans, to "people of color," to being, once again, "colored people." (The linguistic trend toward condensation is strong.) I don't mind any of the names myself. But I have to confess that I like "colored" best, maybe because when I hear the word, I hear it in my mother's voice and in the sepia tones of my childhood. As artlessly and honestly as I can, I have tried to evoke a colored world of the fifties, a Negro world of the early sixties, and the advent of a black world of the later sixties, from the point of view of the boy I was. When you are old enough to read what follows, I hope that it brings you even a small measure of understanding, at long last, of why we see the world with such different eyes . . . and why that is for me a source both of gladness and of regret. And I hope you'll understand why I continue to speak to colored people I pass on the streets.

Love,
Daddy

You're Short, Besides!

Sucheng Chan

Sucheng Chan is a history professor at the University of California at Santa Barbara. Chan won the 1988 Association for Asian American Studies Award for her book *This Bittersweet Soil: The Chinese in California Agriculture, 1860–1910*. Her autobiographical essay discusses the multidimensional character of her self-identity. It traces the ways in which she has struggled with barriers of prejudice and discrimination related to her own particular race, gender, social class, and physical handicap. Chan focuses on the ways such barriers exist simultaneously, creating a complex society in which individuals have multiple group memberships.

When asked to write about being a physically handicapped Asian American woman, I considered it an insult. After all, my accomplishments are many, yet I was not asked to write about any of them. Is being handicapped the most salient feature about me? The fact that it might be in the eyes of others made me decide to write the essay as requested. I realized that the way I think about myself may differ considerably from the way others perceive me. And maybe that's what being physically handicapped is all about.

I was stricken simultaneously with pneumonia and polio at the age of four. Uncertain whether I had polio of the lungs, seven of the eight doctors who attended me—all practitioners of Western medicine—told my parents they should not feel optimistic about my survival. A Chinese fortune teller my mother consulted also gave a grim prognosis, but for an entirely different reason: I had been stricken because my name was offensive to the gods. My grandmother had named me "grandchild of wisdom," a name that the fortune teller said was too presumptuous for a girl. So he advised my parents to change my name to "chaste virgin." All these pessimistic predictions notwithstanding, I hung onto life, if only by a thread. For three years, my body was periodically pierced with electric shocks as the muscles of my legs atrophied. Before my illness, I had been an active, rambunctious, precocious, and very curious child. Being confined to bed was thus a mental agony as great as my physical pain. Living in war-torn China, I received little medical attention; physical therapy was

Excerpted from Sucheng Chan, "You're Short, Besides!," in *Making Waves: An Anthology of Writings By and About Asian American Women*, edited by Asian Women United of California. Reprinted with permission from the author.

unheard of. But I was determined to walk. So one day, when I was six or seven, I instructed my mother to set up two rows of chairs to face each other so that I could use them as I would parallel bars. I attempted to walk by holding my body up and moving it forward with my arms while dragging my legs along behind. Each time I fell, my mother gasped, but I badgered her until she let me try again. After four nonambulatory years, I finally walked once more by pressing my hands against my thighs so my knees wouldn't buckle.

My father had been away from home during most of those years because of the war. When he returned, I had to confront the guilt he felt about my condition. In many East Asian cultures, there is a strong folk belief that a person's physical state in this life is a reflection of how morally or sinfully he or she lived in previous lives. Furthermore, because of the tendency to view the family as a single unit, it is believed that the fate of one member can be caused by the behavior of another. Some of my father's relatives told him that my illness had doubtless been caused by the wild carousing he did in his youth. A well-meaning but somewhat simple man, my father believed them.

Throughout my childhood, he sometimes apologized to me for having to suffer retribution for his former bad behavior. This upset me; it was bad enough that I had to deal with the anguish of not being able to walk, but to have to assuage his guilt as well was a real burden! In other ways, my father was very good to me. He took me out often, carrying me on his shoulders or back, to give me fresh air and sunshine. He did this until I was too large and heavy for him to carry. And ever since I can remember, he has told me that I am pretty. . . .

During my fourth year as an assistant professor at the University of California at Berkeley, I won a distinguished teaching award. Some weeks later I ran into a former professor who congratulated me enthusiastically. But I said to him, "You know what? I became a distinguished teacher by limping across the stage of Dwinelle 155!" (Dwinelle 155 is a large, cold classroom that most colleagues of mine hate to teach in.) I was rude not because I lacked graciousness but because this man, who had told me that my dissertation was the finest piece of work he had read in fifteen years, had nevertheless advised me to eschew a teaching career.

"Why?" I asked. "Your leg . . ." he responded.

"What about my leg?" I said, puzzled.

"Well, how would you feel standing in front of a large lecture class?"

"If it makes any difference, I want you to know I've won a number of speech contests in my life, and I am not the least bit self-conscious about speaking in front of large audiences. . . . Look, why don't you write me a letter of recommendation to tell people how brilliant I am, and let *me* worry about my leg!"

This incident is worth recounting only because it illustrates a dilemma that handicapped persons face frequently: those who care about us sometimes get so protective that they unwittingly limit our growth. This former professor of mine had been one of my greatest supporters for two decades. Time after time, he had written glowing letters of recommendation on my behalf. He had spoken as he did because he thought he had my best interests at heart; he thought that if I got a desk job rather than one that required me to be a visible, public person, I would be spared the misery of being stared at.

Americans, for the most part, do not believe as Asians do that physically handicapped persons are morally flawed. But they are equally inept at interacting with those of us who are not able-bodied. Cultural differences in the perception and treatment of handicapped people are most clearly expressed by adults. Children, regardless of where they are, tend to be openly curious about people who do not look "normal." Adults in Asia have no hesitation in asking visibly handicapped people what is wrong with them, often expressing their sympathy with looks of pity, whereas adults in the United States try desperately to be polite by pretending not to notice.

One interesting response I often elicited from people in Asia but have never encountered in America is the attempt to link my physical condition to the state of my soul. Many a time while living and traveling in Asia people would ask me what religion I belonged to. I would tell them that my mother is a devout Buddhist, that my father was baptized a Catholic but has never practiced Catholicism, and that I am an agnostic. Upon hearing this, people would try strenuously to convert me to their religion so that whichever God they believed in could bless me. If I would only attend this church or that temple regularly, they urged, I would surely get cured. Catholics and Buddhists alike have pressed religious medallions into my palm, telling me if I would wear these, the relevant deity or saint would make me well. Once while visiting the tomb of Muhammad Ali Jinnah in Karachi, Pakistan, an old Muslim, after finishing his evening prayers, spotted me, gestured toward my legs, raised his arms heavenward, and began a new round of prayers, apparently on my behalf.

In the United States adults who try to act "civilized" towards handicapped people by pretending they don't notice anything unusual sometimes end up ignoring handicapped people completely. In the first few months I lived in this country, I was struck by the fact that whenever children asked me what was the matter with my leg, their adult companions would hurriedly shush them up, furtively look at me, mumble apologies, and rush their children away. After a few months of such encounters, I decided it was my responsibility to educate these people. So I would say to the flustered adults, "It's okay, let the kid ask." Turning to the child, I would say, "When I was a little girl, no bigger than you are, I became sick with something called polio. The muscles in my leg shrank up and I couldn't walk very well. You're much luckier than I am because now you can get a vaccine to make sure you never get my disease. So don't cry when your mommy takes you to get a polio vaccine, okay?" Some adults and their little companions I talked to this way were glad to be rescued from embarrassment; others thought I was strange.

Americans have another way of covering up their uneasiness: they become jovially patronizing. Sometimes when people spot my crutch, they ask if I've had a skiing accident. When I answer that unfortunately it is something less glamorous than that, they say, "I bet you *could* ski if you put your mind to it!" Alternately, at parties where people dance, men who ask me to dance with them get almost belligerent when I decline their invitation. They say, "Of course you can dance if you *want* to!" Some have given me pep talks about how if I would only develop the right mental attitude, I would have more fun in life.

Different cultural attitudes toward handicapped persons came out clearly during my wedding. My father-in-law, as solid a representative of middle America as could be found, had no qualms about objecting to the marriage on racial grounds, but he could bring himself to comment on my handicap only indirectly. He wondered why his son, who had dated numerous high school and college beauty queens, couldn't marry one of them instead of me. My mother-in-law, a devout Christian, did not share her husband's prejudices, but she worried aloud about whether I could have children. Some Chinese friends of my parents, on the other hand, said that I was lucky to have found such a noble man, one who would marry me despite my handicap. I, for my part, appeared in church in a white lace wedding dress I had designed and made myself—a miniskirt!

How Asian Americans treat me with respect to my handicap tells me a great deal about their degree of acculturation. Recent immigrants behave just like Asians in Asia; those who have been here longer or who grew up in the United States behave more like their white counterparts. I have not encountered any distinctly Asian American pattern of response. What makes the experience of Asian American handicapped people unique is the duality of responses we elicit.

Regardless of racial or cultural background, most handicapped people have to learn to find a balance between the desire to attain physical independence and the need to take care of ourselves by not overtaxing our bodies. In my case, I've had to learn to accept the fact that leading an active life has its price. Between the ages of eight and eighteen, I walked without using crutches or braces but the effort caused my right leg to become badly misaligned. Soon after I came to the United States, I had a series of operations to straighten out the bones of my right leg; afterwards though my leg looked straighter and presumably better, I could no longer walk on my own. Initially my doctors fitted me with a brace, but I found wearing one cumbersome and soon gave it up. I could move around much more easily—and more important, faster—by using one crutch. One orthopedist after another warned me that using a single crutch was a bad practice. They were right. Over the years my spine developed a double-S curve and for the last twenty years I have suffered from severe, chronic back pains, which neither conventional physical therapy nor a lighter work load can eliminate. . . .

I've often wondered if I would have been a different person had I not been physically handicapped. I really don't know, though there is no question that being handicapped has marked me. But at the same time I usually do not *feel* handicapped—and consequently, I do not *act* handicapped. People are therefore less likely to treat me as a handicapped person. There is no doubt, however, that the lives of my parents, sister, husband, other family members, and some close friends have been affected by my physical condition. They have had to learn not to hide me away at home, not to feel embarrassed by how I look or react to people who say silly things to me, and not to resent me for the extra demands my condition makes on them. Perhaps the hardest thing for those who live with handicapped people is to know when and how to offer help. There are no guidelines applicable to all situations. My advice is, when in doubt, ask, but ask in a way that does not smack of pity or embarrassment. Most important, please don't talk to us as though we are children.

So, has being physically handicapped been a handicap? It all depends on one's attitude. Some years ago, I told a friend that I had once said to an affirmative action compliance officer (somewhat sardonically since I do not believe in the head count approach to affirmative action) that the institution which employs me is triply lucky because it can count me as nonwhite, female and handicapped. He responded, "Why don't you tell them to count you four times? . . . Remember, you're short, besides!"

NATIVE AMERICAN CHILDHOOD MEMORIES

N. Scott Momaday

Native American writer N. Scott Momaday won the 1969 Pulitzer Prize for his novel *House Made of Dawn*. Momaday is considered "the Father of Native American Literature" and has published two collections of poetry: a book of legends from the Kiowa tribe and his autobiography, *The Names*. In this excerpt, Momaday recounts his childhood in New Mexico during the 1940s.

The Jemez Day School was built in 1929. It stood for less than fifty years, not a long life for a building. In the last few years—since my time there—the character of the school changed remarkably. Other buildings grew up around it. The old storerooms, the coalbin, and the garage in which stood the Kohler engine that generated our light and heat, were converted into gleaming modern compartments—a cafeteria, a clinic, bathrooms. The old porch, where my parents and I sat talking or listening to the sounds of the village on summer evenings, became an administrative office, and a kindergarten now stands on the sandy beach where I pastured my horses. No, not a long time. But in that span and in that place were invested many days of my life, and many of the very best, I believe.

My parents hankered after the old, sacred world from which we had come to Hobbs, as I did, too, without clearly knowing it. If you have ever been to the hogans in Canyon de Chelly, or to a squaw dance near Lukachukai—if you have ever heard the riding songs in the dusk, or the music of the *yei bichai*—you will never come away entirely, but a part of you will remain there always; you will have found an old home of the spirit.

It happened that a teaching job opened up at the Cañoncito Day School on the Navajo reservation between Albuquerque and Gallup, and my mother decided to take it. Sooner or later there would be two positions somewhere, my mother was assured, and my father and I would join her. And so it came about, sooner than could have been expected. In a matter of days my parents were offered the two-teacher day school at Jemez Pueblo, some fifty miles north and west of Albuquerque, due west of Santa Fe, in the canyon country beneath the

Reprinted from N. Scott Momaday, "The Names," in *Visions of America: Personal Narratives from the Promised Land*, edited by Wesley Brown and Amy Ling. Reprinted with permission from the author.

Jemez Mountains. None of us had ever been there before. My mother went there directly from Cañoncito, and my father and I collected our things and set out from Hobbs with a man whom my father had hired to move us in his truck. That was in September, 1946. We arrived late at night, having got lost and gone nearly to Cuba, New Mexico, on the Farmington road. I can still see that dirt and gravel road in the light of the headlamps, white, with the black night on either side, the blue, black-dotted dunes in the moonlight beyond, and the bright stars. Rabbits and coyotes crossed the road. There was no pavement then on our way beyond Bernalillo, and for the last thirty miles or so the little truck bounced and rattled into the wild country. I could remember having, years before, when I was small, driven with my father across Snake Flats, on the Navajo. In heavy rain or snow the road was impassable, and we had had to wait until late at night, when it was frozen hard, in order to drive upon it.

The next morning I woke up, and there was a great excitement in me, as if something strange and wonderful had happened in the night: I had somehow got myself deep into the world, deeper than ever before. Perhaps I really expected nothing, and so I could not have been disappointed, but I do not believe that. Anyway, no expectation could possibly have been equal to the brilliance and exhilaration of that autumn New Mexican morning. Outside I caught my breath on the cold, delicious air of the Jemez Valley, lying out at six thousand feet. Around me were all the colors of the earth that I have ever seen. As I think back to that morning, there comes to my mind a sentence in [a novel by Danish writer] Isak Dinesen: "In the highlands you woke up in the morning and thought: Here I am, where I ought to be."

The valley slopes down from north to south, and the pueblo lies down in the depth of it, on the east bank of the shallow Jemez River. Some four miles to the north is the little settlement of Cañon, nestled in sheer formations of red rock, and beyond is the long, deep San Diego Canyon, rising sharply up to the dark-timbered walls of the Jemez Range, to the Valle Grande, which is the largest caldera in the world, and to the summit above eleven thousand feet, from which you can look across the distance eastward to the Sangre de Cristos. Five miles to the south is the village of San Ysidro, where the valley loses its definition and the earth fans out in wide reaches of white, semi-arid plains. The junction at San Ysidro is as close as you can come to Jemez Pueblo in a Trailways bus; State Road 44 runs south and east to Bernalillo, north and west to Cuba, Bloomfield, and Farmington, near my old home of Shiprock. The east side of the valley is a long blue mesa, which from the pueblo seems far away, and in my years there I never covered the whole distance between, though I rode around for a thousand miles, it may be, on horseback. The conformation of that mesa is the rule of a solar calendar; for as long as anyone knows the Jemez people have lived their lives according to the ranging of the sun as it appears every day on that long, level skyline. Closer on the west, across the river, the valley is sharp-edged, given up abruptly to a high, broken wall—to walls beyond walls—of many colors. There is the red mesa upon which are still to be found the ancient ruins of Zia, there the white sandstone cliffs in which is carved the old sacred cave of the Jemez Snake Clan, and there are pink and purple hills, ascending to the lone blue mountain in the northwest, where there are bears and mountain lions as well as deer and where once, in living memory, there were wolves.

The character of the landscape changed from hour to hour in the day, and from day to day, season to season. Nothing there of the earth could be taken for granted; you felt that Creation was going on in your sight. You see things in the high air that you do not see farther down in the lowlands. In the plains you can see farther than you have ever seen, and that is to gain a great freedom. But in the high country all objects bear upon you, and you touch hard upon the earth. The air of the mountains is itself an element in which vision is made acute; eagles bear me out. From my home of Jemez I could see the huge, billowing clouds above the Valle Grande, how, even motionless, they drew close upon me and merged with my life.

At that time the pueblo numbered about a thousand inhabitants. It was then a very close, integrated community, concentrated upon the plaza, with narrow streets and a number of buildings, in each of which several families lived. The population thinned out in proportion as you moved away from the plaza, though there were many *ranchitos,* especially on the north and west, where the fields were numerous. A few families kept houses across the river in order to be near the farthest fields, and in the summer they journeyed there in wagons and set themselves up, but when the harvest was in they returned to the village. It is a principle of their lives that the pueblo people move ever towards the center. Their sacred ceremonies are performed in the plaza, and in the kiva there. On the surrounding edge of the pueblo were numerous corrals, orchards, and little gardens of corn, chili, melons, and squash. In the autumn, and most of all in the late afternoons, the sun set a wonderful glow upon the adobe walls, in the colors of copper and gold, and brilliant red strings of chilies hung from the vigas. There was no electricity at Jemez in 1946, and no water in the village, other than that which was pumped from the ground by means of windmills, three or four in all. The men diverted water from the river for their fields; all about the farmlands was an intricate network of irrigation ditches. And of course much depended upon the rains, and the snowfalls in the mountains. Water is a holy thing in the pueblos; you come to understand there how the heart yearns for it. You learn to watch the level of the river, and when the rain comes, you hold your face and your hands up to it. There were perhaps three pickup trucks in the pueblo then, and no automobiles that I can remember. Everyone went abroad in wagons and on horseback, or else they walked; and frequently the boys and men, even the very young and the very old, ran about on their feet. The pueblo men have always been very good long-distance runners.

By car, unless you happened to come on the old road from San Ysidro, which was by and large a horse-and-wagon path, you entered the pueblo on the east side, on a street (that word is not entirely appropriate—"street," as Americans in cities and suburbs think of that word, does not truly indicate any of the ancient ways of that place, but it will have to do) which curved around the front of the Pueblo Church. The church was a large adobe building with three old Spanish bells in the façade and a burial ground in the yard. The Roman Catholic churches of the pueblos are so old, many of them, that they seem scarcely to impose an alien aspect upon the native culture; rather, they seem themselves almost to have been appropriated by that culture and to express it in its own terms. The church at Jemez has not the rich, rude beauty of the ruin at Acoma, or of even the church at Zia, say; nonetheless there is considerable strength and dignity in it. The extant parish records go back to 1720.

There you came to a fork. If you continued on around the church you were on the way to the San Diego Mission, which lay out on the west side of the village; there was the mission school, which went through the first eight grades, the residence house of the nuns who taught there, the rectory with its adjoining chapel, where lived the Franciscan parish priest and his assistants, and the United States Post Office. If you bore to the left you were on the way to the Jemez Day School, on the southwestern corner of the pueblo, and on the old wagon road to San Ysidro.

The day school was a large stucco building in the pueblo style, not unlike the Pueblo Church in certain respects, especially that part of it which was officially the "school"; it had vigas, a dozen large windows along the south wall, admitting light into the classrooms, and a belfry in front. The two classrooms, situated end to end, were of about the same size; each could accommodate about thirty pupils comfortably. The highest enrollment during my parents' tenure there was sixty-eight. The front classroom was my mother's; she taught the beginners (who comprised a kind of kindergarten class, and most of whom could not speak English when they came), the first, the second, and the third graders. In the other classroom my father, who was the principal, taught the fourth, fifth, and sixth graders. My parents were assisted by a "housekeeper," a Jemez woman whose job it was to clean the classrooms, supervise the playground, and prepare the noon meal for the children. Frequently she assisted as an interpreter as well. On the opposite side of the building were the teachers' quarters, roughly equivalent in size to one of the classrooms. There were a living room, a kitchen, two bedrooms, and a bath. There was also a screened porch in front, where it was comfortable to sit in the good weather, and another, much smaller, in back; the latter we used largely for storage; there was our woodbox, convenient to the living room, in which there was a fireplace, and to the kitchen, in which, when we moved there, there was an old wood-burning range. In the living room there was a door which opened upon my mother's classroom, and beside this door a wall telephone with two bells and a crank. We shared a party line with the San Diego Mission and the Jemez Trading Post; there were no other telephones in the pueblo; we answered to two long rings and one short.

There were two other buildings on the school grounds. In one of these was the garage, a storeroom, the coalbin, and a makeshift clinic to which Government Service doctors and nurses came periodically to treat the ailing people of the village; in the other there lived at various times chickens, ducks, and turkeys—and for some months the meanest rooster I have ever known; perhaps his name was Oliver Blount, or Thaddeus Waring. Once, after he had attacked me viciously, I knocked him unconscious with a stone. It was a lucky throw, through the fence, and the cowardice of it lay heavy on me for days afterwards. Oh, you are a mean one, Blount, but you are not so mean as I.

A white fence encircled the school. We had in back a windmill and a water tank, and beyond the white fence there was a large field where later my father and I built a corral and shelter for Pecos, my strawberry roan quarter horse, my darling, my delight. The grounds were bare at first, except for five elms which shaded the teacherage, but later my mother planted tamaracks and Russian olives along the fence; they flourished. Along the north side of the day school ran the road to the river, which was about a half mile west, and upon that road we saw much of the commerce of the village from our kitchen windows. And just across that road lived our closest neighbors, the Tosa family.

I resumed my seventh-grade studies at the mission school. I loved to walk there in the morning, for on the way there were interesting and beautiful things to see. The old man Francisco Tosa kept a flock of sheep, and as I passed by his corrals I often saw him there, tending them. He always greeted me heartily in Spanish, and there was much good humor in him. There are certain people whom you are simply glad to see at any moment, anywhere, for they hold themselves to their lives very peacefully and know who they are, and Francisco Tosa was one of these. He wore a red kerchief around his head, his long white hair tied with a finely woven band in a queue, and over this a big straw hat. He cut a very handsome figure, I thought, and he was a medicine man. It is the part of a medicine man to be inscrutable, if not austere—or so it has always seemed to me—but Francisco did not live up to such an image; he was jovial and serene, and he personified some old, preeminent ethic of pueblo life. I crossed over a little stream bed, where sometimes there was water, sometimes not; when it was there, animals came to drink, and the women washed corn in their yucca baskets. I passed through a lovely orchard near a house in which I liked to imagine there lived a witch; it strikes me that I never saw anyone there, and yet it was a fine old house and well kept; everything about it was in place. And I bent down through strands of barbed wire and was then in the yard of the mission school.

I was in that position of great advantage again, that of being alone among my classmates at home in the English language. From another and more valid point of view, it was a position of disadvantage. I had no real benefit of instruction at the mission school, and consequently I remember very little of what happened during those hours when I sat at my desk, listening to the nuns. One day Sister Mary Teresa put us the question "Which country is larger, the United States or the Soviet Union?" Child's play. Called upon, I replied confidently that the Soviet Union was certainly the larger country. "No," said Sister Mary Teresa, "the United States is quite a lot bigger than the Soviet Union." And to prove her point she held up two maps, one of each country, which bore no relation to each other in terms of scale; but the two countries were there irrefutably juxtaposed in our sight, and sure enough, the United States appeared to be larger by a third than the Soviet Union. The force of this logic made a great impression on me, and I have not forgotten it. There was a little parable on the nature of faith, I believe; it was as if I had been witness to a miracle.

GROWING UP ASIAN IN AMERICA

Kesaya E. Noda

In this article, Kesaya E. Noda allows the reader to enter into her complex world in which race, gender, and social class intersect to shape her everyday life. Noda's creative writing is representative of an emerging literature by Asian American women. Noda's "coming of age" story reveals universal themes in a young girl's childhood set against Noda's Japanese cultural background.

Sometimes when I was growing up, my identity seemed to hurtle toward me and paste itself right to my face. I felt that way, encountering the stereotypes of my race perpetuated by non-Japanese people (primarily white) who may or may not have had contact with other Japanese in America. "You don't like cheese, do you?" someone would ask. "I know your people don't like cheese." Sometimes questions came making allusions to history. That was another aspect of the identity. Events that had happened quite apart from the me who stood silent in that moment connected my face with an incomprehensible past. "Your parents were in California? Were they in those camps during the war?" And sometimes there were phrases or nicknames: "Lotus Blossom." I was sometimes addressed or referred to as racially Japanese, sometimes as Japanese American, and sometimes as an Asian woman. Confusions and distortions abounded.

How is one to know and define oneself? From the inside—within a context that is self defined, from a grounding in community and a connection with culture and history that are comfortably accepted? Or from the outside—in terms of messages received from the media and people who are often ignorant? Even as an adult I can still see two sides of my face and past. I can see from the inside out, in freedom. And I can see from the outside in, driven by the old voices of childhood and lost in anger and fear.

I Am Racially Japanese

A voice from my childhood says: "You are other. You are less than. You are unalterably alien." This voice has its own history. We have indeed been seen as other and alien since the early years of our arrival in the United States. The very first immigrants were welcomed and

Excerpted from Kesaya Noda, "Growing Up Asian in America," in *Making Waves: An Anthology of Writings By and About Asian Women*, edited by Asian Women United of California. Reprinted with permission from the author.

sought as laborers to replace the dwindling numbers of Chinese, whose influx had been cut off by the Chinese Exclusion Act of 1882. The Japanese fell natural heir to the same anti-Asian prejudice that had arisen against the Chinese. As soon as they began striking for better wages, they were no longer welcomed.

I can see myself today as a person historically defined by law and custom as being forever alien. Being neither "free white," nor "African," our people in California were deemed "aliens, ineligible for citizenship," no matter how long they intended to stay here. Aliens ineligible for citizenship were prohibited from owning, buying, or leasing land. They did not and could not belong here. The voice in me remembers that I am always a *Japanese* American in the eyes of many. A third-generation German American is an American. A third-generation Japanese American is a Japanese American. Being Japanese means being a danger to the country during the war and knowing how to use chopsticks. I wear this history on my face.

I move to the other side. I see a different light and claim a different context. My race is a line that stretches across ocean and time to link me to the shrine where my grandmother was raised. Two high, white banners lift in the wind at the top of the stone steps leading to the shrine. It is time for the summer festival. Black characters are written against the sky as boldly as the clouds, as lightly as kites, as sharply as the big black crows I used to see above the fields in New Hampshire. At festival time there is liquor and food, ritual, discipline, and abandonment. There is music and drunkenness and invocation. There is hope. Another season has come. Another season has gone.

I am racially Japanese. I have a certain claim to this crazy place where the prayers intoned by a neighboring Shinto priest (standing in for my grandmother's nephew who is sick) are drowned out by the rehearsals for the pop singing contest in which most of the villagers will compete later that night. The village elders, the priest, and I stand respectfully upon the immaculate, shining wooden floor of the outer shrine, bowing our heads before the hidden powers. During the patchy intervals when I can hear him, I notice the priest has a stutter. His voice flutters up to my ears only occasionally because two men and a woman are singing gustily into a microphone in the compound, testing the sound system. A prerecorded tape of guitars, samisens, and drums accompanies them. Rock music and Shinto prayers. That night, to loud applause and cheers, a young man is given the award for the most *netsuretsu*—passionate, burning—rendition of a song. We roar our approval of the reward. Never mind that his voice had wandered and slid, now slightly above, now slightly below the given line of the melody. Netsuretsu. Netsuretsu.

In the morning, my grandmother's sister kneels at the foot of the stone stairs to offer her morning prayers. She is too crippled to climb the stairs, so each morning she kneels here upon the path. She shuts her eyes for a few seconds, her motions as matter of fact as when she washes rice. I linger longer than she does, so reluctant to leave, savoring the connection I feel with my grandmother in America, the past, and the power that lives and shines in the morning sun.

Our family has served this shrine for generations. The family's need to protect this claim to identity and place outweighs any individual claim to any individual hope. I am Japanese.

I Am a Japanese American

"Weak." I hear the voice from my childhood years. "Passive," I hear. Our parents and grandparents were the ones who were put into those camps. They went without resistance; they offered cooperation as proof of loyalty to America. "Victim," I hear. And, "Silent."

Our parents are painted as hard workers who were socially uncomfortable and had difficulty expressing even the smallest opinion. Clean, quiet, motivated, and determined to match the American way; that is us, and that is the story of our time here.

"Why did you go into those camps," I raged at my parents, frightened by my own inner silence and timidity. "Why didn't you do anything to resist? Why didn't you name it the injustice it was?" Couldn't our parents even think? Couldn't they? Why were we so passive?

I shift my vision and my stance. I am in California. My uncle is in the midst of the sweet potato harvest. He is pressed, trying to get the harvesting crews onto the field as quickly as possible, worried about the flow of equipment and people. His big pickup is pulled off to the side, motor running, door ajar. I see two tractors in the yard in front of an old shed; the flat bed harvesting platform on which the workers will stand has already been brought over from the other field. It's early morning. The workers stand loosely grouped and at ease, but my uncle looks as harried and tense as a police officer trying to unsnarl a New York City traffic jam. Driving toward the shed, I pull my car off the road to make way for an approaching tractor. The front wheels of the car sink luxuriously into the soft, white sand by the roadside and the car slides to a dreamy halt, tail still on the road. I try to move forward. I try to move back. The front bites contentedly into the sand, the back lifts itself at a jaunty angle. My uncle sees me and storms down the road, running. He is shouting before he is even near me.

"What's the matter with you," he screams. "What the hell are you doing?" In his frenzy, he grabs his hat off his head and slashes it through the air across his knee. He is beside himself. "Don't you know how to drive in sand? What's the matter with you? You've blocked the whole roadway. How am I supposed to get my tractors out of here? Can't you use your head? You've cut off the whole roadway, and we've got to get out of here."

I stand on the road before him helplessly thinking, "No, I don't know how to drive in sand. I've never driven in sand."

"I'm sorry, uncle," I say, burying a smile beneath a look of sincere apology. I notice my deep amusement and my affection for him with great curiosity. I am usually devastated by anger. Not this time.

During the several years that follow I learn about the people and the place, and much more about what has happened in this California village where my parents grew up. The issei, our grandparents, made this settlement in the desert. Their first crops were eaten by rabbits and ravaged by insects. The land was so barren that men walking from house to house sometimes got lost. Women came here too. They bore children in 114 degree heat, then carried the babies with them into the fields to nurse when they reached the end of each row of grapes or other truck farm crops.

I had had no idea what it meant to buy this kind of land and make it grow green. Or how, when the war came, there was no space at all for the subtlety of being who we were—Japanese Americans. Either/or was the way. I hadn't understood that people were literally afraid for their lives then, that their money had been frozen in banks; that there was a five-mile travel limit; that when the early evening curfew came and they were inside their houses, some of them watched helplessly as people they knew went into their barns to steal their belongings. The police were patrolling the road, interested only in violators of curfew. There was no help for them in the face of thievery. I had not been able to imagine before what it must have felt like to be an American—to know absolutely that one is an American—and yet to have almost everyone else deny it. Not only deny it, but challenge that identity with machine guns and troops of white American soldiers. In those circumstances it was difficult to say, "I'm a Japanese American." "American" had to do.

But now I can say that I am a Japanese American. It means I have a place here in this country, too. I have a place here on the East Coast, where our neighbor is so much a part of our family that my mother never passes her house at night without glancing at the lights to see if she is home and safe; where my parents have hauled hundreds of pounds of rocks from fields and arduously planted Christmas trees and blueberries, lilacs, asparagus, and crab apples; where my father still dreams of angling a stream to a new bed so that he can dig a pond in the field and fill it with water and fish. "The neighbors already came for their Christmas tree?" he asks in December. "Did they like it? Did they like it?"

I have a place on the West Coast where my relatives still farm, where I heard the stories of feuds and backbiting, and where I saw that people survived and flourished because fundamentally they trusted and relied upon one another. A death in the family is not just a death in a family; it is a death in the community. I saw people help each other with money, materials, labor, attention, and time. I saw men gather once a year, without fail, to clean the grounds of a ninety-year-old woman who had helped the community before, during, and after the war. I saw her remembering them with birthday cards sent to each of their children.

I come from a people with a long memory and a distinctive grace. We live our thanks. And we are Americans. Japanese Americans.

I Am a Japanese American Woman

Woman. The last piece of my identity. It has been easier by far for me to know myself in Japan and to see my place in America than it has been to accept my line of connection with my own mother. She was my dark self, a figure in whom I thought I saw all that I feared most in myself. Growing into womanhood and looking for some model of strength, I turned away from her. Of course, I could not find what I sought. I was looking for a black feminist or a white feminist. My mother is neither white nor black.

My mother is a woman who speaks with her life as much as with her tongue. I think of her with her own mother. Grandmother had Parkinson's disease and it had frozen her gait and set her fingers, tongue, and feet jerking and trembling in a terrible dance. My aunts and uncles wanted her to be able to live in her own home. They fed her, bathed her, dressed her, awoke at midnight to take her for one last trip to the bathroom. My aunts (her daughters-in-law) did most of the care, but my mother went from New Hampshire to California each summer to spend a month living with grandmother, because she wanted to and because she wanted to give my aunts at least a small rest. During those hot summer days, mother lay on the couch watching the television or reading, cooking foods that grandmother liked, and speaking little. Grandmother thrived under her care.

The time finally came when it was too dangerous for grandmother to live alone. My relatives kept finding her on the floor beside her bed when they went to wake her in the mornings. My mother flew to California to help clean the house and make arrangements for grandmother to enter a local nursing home. On her last day at home, while grandmother was sitting in her big, overstuffed armchair, hair combed and wearing a green summer dress, my mother went to her and knelt at her feet. "Here, Mamma," she said. "I've polished your shoes." She lifted grandmother's legs and helped her into the shiny black shoes. My grandmother looked down and smiled slightly. She left her house walking, supported by her children, carrying her pocket book, and wearing her polished black shoes. "Look, Mamma," my mom had said, kneeling. "I've polished your shoes."

Just the other day, my mother came to Boston to visit. She had recently lost a lot of weight and was pleased with her new shape and her feeling of good health. "Look at me, Kes," she exclaimed, turning toward me, front and back, as naked as the day she was born. I saw her small breasts and the wide, brown scar, belly button to pubic hair, that marked her because my brother and I were both born by Caesarean section. Her hips were small. I was not a large baby, but there was so little room for me in her that when she was carrying me she could not even begin to bend over toward the floor. She hated it, she said.

"Don't I look good? Don't you think I look good?"

I looked at my mother, smiling and as happy as she, thinking of all the times I have seen her naked. I have seen both my parents naked throughout my life, as they have seen me. From childhood through adulthood we've had our naked moments, sharing baths, idle conversations picked up as we moved between showers and closets, hurried moments at the beginning of days, quiet moments at the end of days.

I know this to be Japanese, this ease with the physical, and it makes me think of an old, Japanese folk song. A young nursemaid, a fifteen-year-old girl, is singing a lullaby to a baby who is strapped to her back. The nursemaid has been sent as a servant to a place far from her own home. "We're the beggars," she says, "and they are the nice people. Nice people wear fine sashes. Nice clothes."

> If I should drop dead,
> bury me by the roadside!
> I'll give a flower
> to everyone who passes.

> What kind of flower?
> The cam-cam-camellia [tsun-tsun-tsubaki]
> watered by Heaven:
> alms water.

The nursemaid is the intersection of heaven and earth, the intersection of the human, the natural world, the body, and the soul. In this song, with clear eyes, she looks steadily at life, which is sometimes so very terrible and said. I think of her while looking at my mother, who is standing on the red and purple carpet before me, laughing, without any clothes.

I am my mother's daughter. And I am myself.

I am a Japanese American woman.

I recently heard a man from West Africa share some memories of his childhood. He was raised Muslim, but when he was a young man, he found himself deeply drawn to Christianity. He struggled against this inner impulse for years, trying to avoid the church yet feeling pushed to return to it again and again. "I would have done *anything* to avoid the change," he said. At last, he became Christian. Afterwards he was afraid to go home, fearing that he would not be accepted. The fear was groundless, he discovered, when at last he returned—he had separated himself, but his family and friends (all Muslim) had not separated themselves from him.

The man, who is now a professor of religion, said that in the Africa he knew as a child and a young man, pluralism was embraced rather than feared. There was "a kind of tolerance that did not deny your particularity," he said. He alluded to zestful, spontaneous debates that would sometimes loudly erupt between Muslims and Christians in the village's public spaces. His memories of an atheist who harangued the villagers when he came to visit them once a week moved me deeply. Perhaps the man was an agricultural advisor or inspector. He harassed the women. He would say:

> "Don't go to the fields! Don't even bother to go to the fields. Let God take care of you. He'll send you the food. If you believe in God, why do you need to work? You don't need to work! Let God put the seeds in the ground. Stay home."

The professor said, "The women laughed, you know? They just laughed. Their attitude was, 'Here is a child of God. When will he come home?'"

The storyteller, the professor of religion, smiled a most fantastic, tender smile as he told his story. "In my country, there is a deep affirmation of the oneness of God," he said. "The atheist and the women were having quite different experiences in their encounter, though the atheist did not know this. He saw himself as quite separate from the women. But the women did not see themselves as being separate from him. 'Here is a child of God,' they said. 'When will he come home?'"

Growing Up Chicana

Olivia Castellano

A writer and professor at California State University at Sacramento, Olivia Castellano recalls her childhood along the Texas-Mexico border. Castellano analyzes her experiences as a student within the American educational system. She also examines her struggles as a university professor and the type of teaching styles that she has adopted in her multicultural classrooms.

In Comstock, the Tex-Mex border town about 15 miles from the Rio Grande where I spent the first 12 years of my life, I saw the despair that poverty and hopelessness had etched in the faces of young Chicano men who, like my father, walked back and forth on the dusty path between Comstock and the Southern Pacific Railroad station. They would set out every day on rail carts to repair the railroad. The women of Comstock fared no better. Most married early, I had seen them in their kitchens toiling at the stove, with one baby propped on one hip and two toddlers tugging at their skirts. Or, they followed their working mothers' route, cleaning house and doing laundry for rich Texan ranchers who paid them a pittance. I decided very early that this was not the future I wanted.

In 1958 my father, tired of seeing days fade into each other without promise, moved us to California, where we became farmworkers in the San Jose area (then a major agricultural center). I saw the same futile look in the faces of young Chicanos and Chicanas working beside my family. Those faces already lined so young with sadness made me deadly serious about my books and my education.

At a young age—between 11 and 14—I began my intellectual and spiritual rebellion against my parents and society. I fell in love with books and created space of my own where I could dare to dream. Yet, in school I remained shy and introverted, terrified of my white male professors. In my adolescence, I rebelled against my mother's insistence that Mexican girls should marry young, as she did at 18. But, I didn't care if my cousins Alicia and Anita were getting married and having babies early. "I was put on this earth to make books, not babies!" I announced and ran into my room.

Books became my obsession. I wanted to read everything that I was

Reprinted from Olivia Castellano, "Canto, locura y poesia," *Women's Review of Books*, vol. 7, no. 5, February 1990. Reprinted with permission from the author.

not supposed to. By 14 I was already getting to know the Marquis de Sade, Rimbaud, Lautréamont, Whitman, Dostoyevsky, Marx. I came by these writers serendipitously. To get from home to Sacramento High School, I had to walk through one of the toughest neighborhoods in the city, Oak Park. There were men hanging out with liquor in brown paper bags, playing dice, shooting craps and calling from cars: "Hey, baby, get in here with me!" I'd run into the small Oak Park Library which turned out to have a little bit of everything. I would walk around staring at the shelves, killing time till the shifty-eyed men would go away.

The librarians knew and tolerated me with skepticism: "Are you sure you're going to read the Marquis de Sade? Do your parents know you're checking out this material? What are you doing with the Communist Manifesto?" One librarian even forbade me to check the books out, so I'd sit in the library reading for hours on end. Later, at 16 or 17, I was allowed to check out anything I wanted.

The librarians gave me *carte blanche* circulation, so it was that I came to grapple with tough language and ideas. These books were hot! Yet I also was obsessed with wanting to be pretty, mysterious, silent and sexy. I wanted to have long curly hair, red lips and long red nails; to wear black tight dresses and high heels. I wanted desperately to look like the sensuous femmes fatales of the Mexican cinema—María Félix, one of the most beautiful and famous of Mexico's screen goddesses, and Libertad Lamarque, the smoky-voiced, green-eyed Argentinian singer. These were the women I admired when my mother and I went to the movies. But these were my "outward" models. My "inward" models, the voices of the intellect that spoke to me when I shut the door to my room, were, as you have gathered, a writer of erotica, two mad surrealists, a crazy Romantic, an epileptic literary genius, and a radical socialist.

I needed to sabotage society in a major, intellectually radical way. I needed to be a warrior who would catch everyone off guard. But to be a warrior, you must never let your opponent figure you out. When the bullets of racism and sexism are flying at you, you must be very clever in deciding how you want to live. I knew that everything around me—school, teachers, television, friends, men, even my own parents, who in their own internalized racism and self-hatred didn't really believe I'd amount to much though they hoped like hell life would prove them wrong—everything was against me and this I understood fully.

To protect myself, I fell in love with Language—all of it, poems, stories, novels, plays, songs, biographies, *cuentos* or little vignettes, movies—all manifestations of spoken and written language. I fell in love with ideas, with essays by writers like Bacon and Montaigne. I began my serious reading crusade around age 11, when I was already convinced that books alone would save my life. Only through them and through songs, I felt, would I be free to shape some kind of future for myself.

I wanted to prove to anyone who cared to ask (though by now I was convinced no one gave a damn) that I, the daughter of a laborer-farmworker, could dare to be somebody. Try to imagine what it is like to be full of rage at everything: at white teachers who could never pronounce my name (I was called anything from "Odilia" to "Otilia" to "Estela"); rage at those teachers who asked me point blank, "But how did you get to be so smart? You are Mexican, aren't you?"; rage at my 11th-grade English teacher who said to me in front of the whole class, "You stick to essay writing; never try to write a poem again because a poet you are not!" (This after I had worked for two diligent weeks on an imitation of "La Belle Dame Sans Merci"! Now I can laugh. Then it was pitiful).

From age 13, I was also angry at boys who hounded me for dates. When I'd reject them they'd yell, "So what do you plan to do for the rest of your life, fuck a book?" Angry at my Chicana classmates in high school who, perhaps jealous of my high grades, would accuse, "What are you trying to do, be like the whites?" And regrettably, I was angry at my parents, exasperated by their docility, their limited expectations of life. I knew they were proud; but sometimes, in their own misdirected rage (maybe afraid of my little successes), they would make painful comments. "Te vas a volver loca con eves jodidos libros" ("You'll go nuts with those damned books") was my mother's frequent warning. Or the even more sickening, "Esta nunca se va a casar." ("Give up on this one; she'll never get married.") This was the tenor of my adolescent years. When nothing on either side of the two cultures, Mexican or Anglo-American, affirms your existence, that is how rage is shaped.

While I managed to escape at least from the obvious entrapments—a teen pregnancy, a destructive early marriage—I did not escape years of being told I wasn't quite right, that because of my ethnicity and gender I was somehow defective, incomplete. Those years left wounds on my self-esteem, wounds so deep that even armed with my books and stolen knowledge I could not entirely escape deep feelings of unworthiness.

By the time I graduated from high school and managed to get a little scholarship to California State University, Sacramento, where I now teach (in 1962 it was called Sacramento State College), I had become very unassertive, immensely shy. I was afraid to look unfeminine if I raised my hand in class, afraid to seem ridiculous if I asked a "bad" question and all eyes turned on me. A deeper part of me was afraid that my rage might rear its ugly head and I would be considered "one more angry Mexican accusing everybody of racism." I was painfully concerned with my physical appearance: wasn't I supposed to look beautiful like Felix and Lamarque? Yet while I wanted to look pretty for the boys, the thought of having sex terrified me. What if I got pregnant, had to quit college and couldn't read my books any more? The more I feared boys, the more I made myself attractive for them, the more they made advances, the more I rejected them.

This constant tension sapped my energy and distracted me from my creative journeys into language. Oh, I would write little things (poems, sketches for stories, journal entries), but I was afraid to show them to anyone. Besides, no one knew I was writing them. I was so frightened by my white, male professors, especially in the English department—they looked so arrogant and were so ungiving of their knowledge that I didn't have the nerve to major in English, though it was the subject I loved.

Instead, I chose to major in French. The "Parisians" and "Québecois" in the French department faculty admired my French accent: "Mademoiselle, êtes-vous certaine que vous n'êtes pas Parisienne?" they would ask. In short, they cared. They engaged me in dialogue, asked why I preferred to study French instead of Spanish ("I already know Spanish," I'd say.) So French became my adopted language. I could play with it, sing songs in it and sound exotic. It complemented my Spanish; besides, I didn't have to worry about speaking English with my heavy Spanish accent and risk being ridiculed. At one point, my spoken French was better than my oral Spanish and my written French has remained better than my written Spanish.

Thus, at 23, armed with a secondary school teaching credential and a B.A. in French with an English minor, I became a high school teacher of French and English. Soon after that, I began to work for a school district where the majority of the students were Chicanos and Blacks from families on welfare and/or from households run by women.

After two years of high school teaching, I returned to Cal State at Sacramento for the Master's degree. Professionally and artistically, it was the best decision I have ever made. The Master's program in which I was accepted was a pilot program in its second year at CSU Sacramento. Called the "Mexican American Experienced Teachers Fellowship," it was run by a team of anthropology professors, central among whom was Professor Steven Arvizu. The program was designed to turn us graduates into "agents of social change." It was 1969 and this was one of the first federally funded (Title V) programs to address Mexican-American students' needs by re-educating their teachers.

My interests were literary, but all 20 of us "fellows" had to get an M.A. in social anthropology, since this experiment took the "anthropologizing education" approach. We studied social dynamics, psycholinguistics, history of Mexico, history of the American Southwest, community activism, confrontational strategies and the nature of the Chicano Movement. The courses were eye-openers. I had never heard the terms Chicano, biculturalism, marginality, assimilation, Chicanismo, protest art. I had never heard of César Chávez and the farm-workers nor of Luis Valdéz and his Teatro Campesino. I had never studied the nature of racism and identity. The philosophy of the program was that culture is a powerful tool for learning, self-expression, solidarity and positive change. Exploring it can help Chicano students understand their bicultural circumstances.

The program brought me face to face with nineteen other Chicano men and women, all experienced public school teachers like myself, with backgrounds like mine. The program challenged every aspect of my life. Through group counseling, group encounter, classroom interaction, course content and community involvement I was allowed to express my rage and to examine it in the company of peers who had a similar anger. Most of our instructors, moreover, were Chicano or white professors sensitive to Chicanos. For the first time, at 25, I had found my role models. I vowed to do for other students what these people had done for me.

Eighteen years of teaching, primarily white women students, Chicanos, and Blacks at California State University, Sacramento have led me to see myself less as a teacher and more as a cultural worker, struggling against society to undo the damage of years of abuse. I continue to see myself as a warrior empowered by my rage. Racism and sexism leave two clear-cut scars on my students: internalized self-hatred and fear of their own creative passion, in my view the two most serious obstacles in the classroom. Confronting this two-headed monster made me razor-sharp. Given their tragic personal stories, the hope in my students' eyes reconfirms daily the incredible beauty, the tenacity of the human spirit.

Teaching white women students (ages 30–45) is no different from working with Chicano and Black students (both men and women): you have to bring about changes in the way they view themselves, their abilities, their right to get educated, and their relation to a world that has systematically oppressed them simply for being who they are. You have to help them channel and understand the seething rage they carry deep inside, a rage which, left unexpressed, can turn them against each other and, more sadly, against themselves. . . .

Mine is a teaching load that, in my early teaching years, used to drive me close to insanity from physical, mental and spiritual exhaustion—spiritual from having internalized my students' pain. Perhaps not fully empowered myself, not fully emplumed in the feather of my own creativity (to borrow the "emplumada" metaphor coined by Lorna Dee Cervantes, the brilliant Chicana poet), I allowed their rage to become part of mine. This kind of rage can kill you. And so through years of working with these kinds of students I have learned to make my spirit strong with "canto, locura y poesia" (song, madness and poetry).

Truly, it takes a conjurer, a magus with all the teaching cards up her sleeve, to deal with the fragmented souls that show up in my classes.

Among the Chicanos and Blacks, I get ex-offenders (mostly men but occasionally a woman who has done time), orphans, single women heads of household, high school dropouts who took years to complete their Graduation Equivalency Diploma.

I get women who have been raped or have been sexually abused either by a father figure or by male relatives—Sylvia Tracey, for example, a 30-year-old Chicana feminist, mother of two, whose parents pressured her to marry her rapist and who is going through divorce after ten years of marriage. I get battered women who are still in a violent marriage or finally got the courage to say enough. And, of course, I get the young Chicano and Black young yuppies who don't believe the world existed before 1970, who know nothing about the sixties' history of struggle and student protest, who—in the case of the Chicanos—feel ashamed that their parents speak English with an accent or were once farmworkers. Most of my students are ashamed of their writing skills and have never once been told that they could succeed in school.

Annetta Jones is typical. A 45-year-old Black woman who single-handedly raised three children, all college-educated and successful, she is still married to a man who served ten years in prison for being a "hit man." She visited him faithfully in prison and underwent all kinds of humiliation at the hands of correctional officers—even granting them sexual favors for conjugal visits with her husband. When her husband completed his time, he fell in love with a young woman from Chicago, where he now lives.

Among my white women students (ranging in age from 25 to 40, though occasionally I get a 45- or 50-year-old "re-entry" woman who wants to be an elementary or high school teacher and "help out young kids so they won't have to go through what I went through"— their exact words) I get women who are either divorced or divorcing; rarely do I get a "happily" married woman. This is especially true of the white women who take my Chicano literature and my credential-pedagogy classes. Take Lynne Trebeck, for instance, a white woman about 40 years old who runs a farm. When she entered the university, her husband objected, so she divorced him! They continue to live in the same house (he refused to leave), "but now he has no control over me," as she told me triumphantly midway through the semester. She has two sons, 15 and 18-years-old; as a young woman, she did jail time as the accomplice of a convicted drug dealer.

Every semester I get two or three white lesbian feminists. This semester there was Vivianne Rose, about 40, in my Chicano literature class. On the first day of class she wore Levi pants, a baggy sweat shirt, white tennis shoes and a beige baseball cap. But, apparently sensing too much conservatism in the students, and knowing that she wanted to be an elementary school teacher, she chose to conceal her sexual orientation. By the end of the first week she had switched to ultrafeminine dresses and flowery skirts, brightly colored blouses, nylons and medium-heeled black shoes, along with lipstick and eye makeup. When she spoke in class she occasionally made references to "my husband who is Native-American." She and Sylvia Tracey became very close friends. Halfway through the course, they informed me that "Shit, it's about time we tell her." (This from Sylvia.) "Oh, hell, why not," Vivianne said; "my husband is a woman." Vivianne Rose lived on a reservation for years and taught Native-American children to read and write. She speaks "Res" (reservation speech) and has adopted her "husband's" last name.

Among my white women students there are also divorced women who are raising two to four children, usually between the ages of eight and seventeen. The most confident are the older, widowed white women who are taking classes for their own enjoyment, not for a degree. They also tell stories of torment: rapes, beatings, verbal and emotional harassment from their men. On occasion, as I said, I get women who have done jail time, usually for taking the rap for drug-connected boyfriends. Among the older married women, the litany echoes again and again: "My husband doesn't really want me in school." "My husband doesn't really care what I do in college as long as I take care of his needs and the kids' needs." "My husband doesn't really know what I'm studying—he has never asked and I've never told him."

Most of the white women as well as the minority students come to the university through special programs. There is the "Educational Opportunity Program" for students who do not meet all university entrance requirements or whose high school grade point average is simply too low for regular admission. The "Student Affirmative Action Program" is for students who need special counseling and tutoring to bring their academic skills up to par or deal with emotional trauma. And the "College Assistance Migrant Program" assists students whose parents are migrant farmworkers in the agricultural areas surrounding the city of Sacramento. There is a wonderful program called PASAR for older women students entering the university for the first time or returning after a multiple-year absence. The Women's Resource Center also provides small grants and scholarships for these re-entry women. A large number of my students (both white and minority women) come severely handicapped in their basic language, math and science skills; a large number have never used a computer. It is not uncommon (especially among Chicanos and Blacks) to get an incoming student who scores at the fifth- and sixth-grade reading levels. Imagine the damage I must help repair!

The task is Herculean, the rewards spiritually fulfilling. I would not have it any other way. Every day is a lesson in humility and audacity. That my students have endured nothing but obstacles and put-downs yet have the courage and strength to seek a college education, humbles me. They are, like me, walking paradoxes. They have won against all the odds (their very presence on campus attests to that). Yet, they haven't won: their deeply ingrained sense of inferiority convinces them that they are not worthy of success.

This is my challenge, I embrace it wholeheartedly. There is no other place I'd rather be, no profession more noble. Sure, I sometimes have doubts; every day something new, sad, even tragic comes up. Just as I was typing this article, for instance, Vicky, one of the white students in my Chicano literature class, called in tears, barely able to talk. "Professor, I can't possibly turn in my paper to your mailbox by four o'clock," she cried. "Everything in my house is falling apart! My husband just fought with my oldest daughter [from a previous marriage], has thrown her out of the house. He's running up and down the street, yelling and threatening to leave us. And I'm sitting here trying to write your paper! I'm going crazy. I feel like walking away from it all!" I took an hour from writing this article to help her contain herself. By the end of our conversation, I had her laughing. I also put her in touch with a counselor friend of mine and gave her a two-day extension for her final paper. And naturally I was one more hour late with my own writing!

I teach in a totally non-traditional way. I use every trick in the book: much positive reinforcement, both oral and written; many one-on-one conferences. I help women develop a network of women with each other, refer them to professor friends who can help them; connect them with graduate students and/or former students who are already pursuing careers. In the classroom, I force students to stand in front of their classmates, to explain concepts or read and evaluate their essays aloud. I create panels representing opposing viewpoints and hold debates—much oral participation, role-playing, reading their own texts. Their own writing and opinions become part of the course. On exams I ask them questions about their classmates' presentations. I meet with individual students in local coffee houses or taverns; it's much easier to talk about personal pain over coffee or a beer or a glass of wine than in my office. My students, for the most part, do not have a network of support outside of the university. There are no supportive husbands, lovers (except on rare occasions, as with my lesbian students), no relatives saying, "Yes, you can do it."

Is it any wonder that when these students enter the university they have a deep sense of personal shame about everything—poor skills, being older students. They are angry at the schools for having prepared them poorly; at their parents for not having had high enough expectations of them or (in the case of the women) for having allowed them to marry so young. Sylvia, my Chicana feminist student, put it best when I was pointing out incomplete sentences in her essay: "Where the hell was I when all this was being taught in high school? And why didn't anybody give a damn that I wasn't learning it?"

I never teach content for the first two weeks of the semester. I talk about anger, sexism, racism and the sixties—a time when people believed in something larger than themselves. I allow them space to talk—about prisons and why so many Chicano and Black young men are behind bars in California; why people fear differences; why our society is gripped by homophobia. I give my students a chance to talk about their anger ("coraje" in Spanish). I often read them a poem by my friend and colleague José Montoya, called "Eslipping and Esliding," in which he talks about "locura" (craziness) and says that with a little locura, a little eslipping and esliding, we can survive the madness that surrounds us. We laugh at ourselves, sharing our tragic, tattered pasts, undoing everything and letting the anger out. "I know why so many of you are afraid of doing well," I say. "You've been told you can't do it, and you're so angry about it, you can't concentrate." Courage takes pure concentration. By the end of these initial two or three weeks we have become friends and defined our mutual respect. Only then do we enter the course content.

I am not good at endings; I prefer to celebrate beginnings. The struggle continues, and the success stories abound. Students come back, year after year, to say "Thank you." Usually, I pull these visitors into the classroom: "Tell my class that they can do it. Tell them how you did it!" The visitors start talking and can't stop. "Look, Olivia, when I first came into your class," said Sylvia, "I couldn't even put a fucking sentence together. And now look at me, three years later I'm even writing poetry!"

RELATED WEBSITES

http://esblibrary.berkeley.edu/eslhome.html

The Ethnic Studies Library provides a guide to major ethnic studies collections at the University of California, Berkeley. Library sites are listed by library holdings of Berkeley's ethnic studies programs, such as Asian American Studies Library.

www.dir.yahoo.com/social_sciences.ethnic_studies

The *social sciences* and *ethnic studies* keywords provide a guide to major ethnic studies links classified by specific academic discipline, such as Native American or Asian American studies. This site includes links to additional websites for organizations and agencies dealing with cultural diversity and ethnic community centers.

www.edu/isd/archives/ethnicstudies/asian

The University of Southern California Asian American Studies Resource Guide includes links to general reference guides, libraries, organizations, audio and video recordings, and periodicals.

www.geocities.com/collegepark.quad.9594

The Guide to AfroAmerican Studies and Community Organizations specializes in links to African American university research centers, biographies of famous African Americans, and other links to educational programs.

www.library.pima.edu

Pima Community College Guide, based out of Tucson, Arizona, specializes in links to *Native American Studies* magazine, periodical databases, and resources in higher education organizations, directories, and databases.

www.sscnet.ucla.edu.csrc

The University of California at Los Angeles Chicano Research Center library collection and archives are the primary national depository for Chicano studies.

www.uga.edu/womanist

Social Sciences and African American Studies includes an index and table of contents to issues of the University of Georgia journal *Womanist Theory and Research*. It specializes in links to other publications on African American women and women in general as well as provides links to feminist scholarship.

BIBLIOGRAPHY

Books

Elliott Robert Barkan, ed.	*A Nation of Peoples: A Sourcebook on America's Multicultural Heritage.* Westport, CT: Greenwood Press, 1999.
Wesley Brown and Amy Ling	*Visions of America: Personal Narratives from the Promised Land.* New York: Persea, 1993.
Irene Browne, ed.	*Latinas and African American Women at Work: Race, Gender, and Economic Inequality.* New York: Russell Sage, 1999.
Sucheng Chan et al.	*Peoples of Color in the American West.* Lexington, MA: D.C. Heath, 1994
Virgina Cyrus	*Experiencing Race, Class, and Gender in the United States.* Mountain View, CA: Mayfield, 1993.
Hien Duc Do	*The Vietnamese Americans.* Westport, CT: Greenwood Press, 1999.
Joe R. Feagin and Clairece Booher Feagin	*Racial and Ethnic Relations.* Upper Saddle River, NJ: Prentice-Hall, 1996.
Miguel Gonzales-Pando	*The Cuban Americans.* Westport, CT: Greenwood Press, 1998.
Woo Moo Hurh	*The Korean Americans.* Westport, CT: Greenwood Press, 1998.
Karen Isaksen Leonard	*The South Asian Americans.* Westport, CT: Greenwood Press, 1997.
Franklin Ng	*The Taiwanese Americans.* Westport, CT: Greenwood Press, 1998.
Suzanne Oboler	*Ethnic Labels, Latino Lives: Identity and the Politics of Representation in the United States.* St. Paul: University of Minnesota, 1995.
Alejandro Portes and Ruben G. Rumbaut	*Immigrant America: A Portrait.* Berkeley and Los Angeles: University of California Press, 1996.
Barbara M. Posadas	*The Filipino Americans.* Westport, CT: Greenwood Press, 1999.
Maria P.P. Root, ed.	*The Multiracial Experience: Racial Borders as the New Frontier.* Thousand Oaks, CA: Sage, 1996.
Renato Rosaldo	*Culture & Truth: The Remaking of Social Analysis.* Boston: Beacon Press, 1997.
Ronald Takaki	*A History of Multicultural America.* New York: Little, Brown, 1994.
Benson Tong	*The Chinese Americans.* Westport, CT: Greenwood Press, 2000.
Silvio Torres-Saillant and Ramona Hernandez	*The Dominican Americans.* Westport, CT: Greenwood Press, 1998.

Periodicals

Richard Alba and
John Logan
"Minority Proximity to Whiteness in the Suburbs,"
American Journal of Sociology, vol. 98, 1993.

David W. Chen
"Asian Middle Class Alters a Rural Enclave," *New York
Times,* December 27, 1999.

David W. Chen
"Indian Tribe Offers Landowners a Conditional Deal,"
New York Times, April 27, 2000.

Ellis Cose
"The Good News About Black America," *Newsweek,*
June 7, 1999.

Jorge Duany
"Reconstructing Racial Identity: Ethnicity, Color, and
Class Among Dominicans in the United States and
Puerto Rico," *Latin American Perspectives,* vol. 25, 1998.

Howard Fineman
"Race and Rage," *Newsweek,* April 3, 1995.

Michael A. Fletcher
"Latinos at the Back of the Class," *Washington Post*
National Weekly Edition, August 10, 1998.

Herbert J. Gans
"Ethnic Invention and Acculturation," Comment,
Journal of American Ethnic History, vol. 12, 1992.

Stephen O. Holmes
"Many Uncertain About President's Racial Effort," *New
York Times,* June 16, 1997.

Stephen O. Holmes
"New Survey Shows Americans Pessimistic on Race
Relations," *New York Times,* June 11, 1997.

Dirk Johnson
"Growth of Gambling on Tribal Lands Starts Trek Back
Home by Indians," *New York Times,* January 17, 1999.

Peter T. Kilborn
"For Poorest Indians, Casinos Aren't Enough," *New
York Times,* June 11, 1997.

Michael Lind
"The Beige and the Black," *New York Times,* August 16,
1998.

Mireya Navarro
"Latinos Gain Visibility in Cultural Life of United
States," *New York Times,* September 19, 1999.

Orlando Patterson
"Ecumenical America: Global Culture and the
American Cosmos," *World Policy Journal,* Summer
1994.

Matthew C. Snipp
"Some Observations About Racial Boundaries and the
Experience of American Indians," *Ethnic and Racial
Studies,* vol. 20, 1997.

Ronald Takaki
"Multiculturalism: Battleground or Meeting Ground?"
Annals of the American Academy, 1993.

Mary C. Waters and
Karl Eschback
"Immigration and Ethnic and Racial Inequality in the
United States," *Annual Review of Sociology,* vol. 20, 1997.

August Wilson
"American Histories: Closing Dreams and Nightmares:
Sailing the Stream of Black Culture," *New York Times,*
April 22, 2000.

Howard Winant
"Racism Today: Continuity and Change in the Post–
Civil Rights Era," *Ethnic and Racial Studies,* vol. 21,
1998.

INDEX